So you really want t

LATIN
PREP

BOOK 2

Answer Book

So you really want to learn

LATIN
PREP

BOOK 2
Answer Book

Theo Zinn M.A. (Oxon.)

Series Editor: Nicholas Oulton M.A. (Oxon.)

www.galorepark.co.uk

GALORE PARK

Published by Galore Park Publishing Ltd,
19/21 Sayers Lane, Tenterden, Kent TN30 6BW
www.galorepark.co.uk

Printed by The Bath Press

ISBN-10: 1 902984 420
ISBN-13: 978 1 902984 42 1

First published 2004
Reprinted 2005

Accompanying this course:

Latin Prep 1 pupil's book	ISBN-10: 1 902984 15 3
Latin Prep 1 answer book	ISBN-10: 1 902984 16 1
Latin Prep 2 pupil's book	ISBN-10: 1 902984 41 2
Latin Prep 2 answer book	ISBN-10: 1 902984 42 0
Latin Prep 3 pupil's book	ISBN-10: 1 902984 36 6
Latin Prep 3 answer book	ISBN-10: 1 902984 43 9

Available in the So you really want to learn series:

English
Latin
French
Maths
Science

Acknowledgements

I remain grateful as ever to Peter and Jackie Fennymore for their continual support and assistance and to Rupert Fennymore for his invaluable help. I should like to express my very special thanks once more to Peter Brown of Trinity College, Oxford for his unending patience and learned approach to problem after problem. And I am particularly grateful to Nicholas Oulton for his very special work in the preparation of this book and to Michael Webb of Northbourne Park School who read the proofs. I need hardly say that all mistakes and infelicities are, once again, entirely my own work.

Preface

This book is devoted solely to giving suggested answers to the exercises set in Latin Prep Book 2. I have not given every possible answer to every question but have tried to produce enough variation in the answers to make clear what alternatives would be acceptable. I have almost always translated the 3rd person singular (not governed by a noun) as 'he', and I have sometimes translated a Latin imperfect by an English simple past - and an English simple past by a Latin imperfect.

It has long been said and widely taught that adjectives in Latin come after the nouns they describe. While tending to stick to what may be called a traditional word order in this regard in the majority of sentences, I have given a very large number of examples of adjectives preceding their nouns, both in the pupil's book and in these suggested answers. The reason for this is that, the more I have looked into the matter, the less evidence have I found to support the belief that adjectives should regularly come after their nouns. I hope to say something about this in Book 3.

TLZ

Chapter 1

Exercise 1.1

1. *lūx, lūcis,* f. = light

	Singular	Plural
Nominative	*lūx*	*lūcēs*
Vocative	*lūx*	*lūcēs*
Accusative	*lūcem*	*lūcēs*
Genitive	*lūcis*	*lūcum*
Dative	*lūcī*	*lūcibus*
Ablative	*lūce*	*lūcibus*

2. *vōx, vōcis,* f. = voice

	Singular	Plural
Nominative	*vōx*	*vōcēs*
Vocative	*vōx*	*vōcēs*
Accusative	*vōcem*	*vōcēs*
Genitive	*vōcis*	*vōcum*
Dative	*vōcī*	*vōcibus*
Ablative	*vōce*	*vōcibus*

3. *dux, ducis,* c. = leader, general, captain

	Singular	Plural
Nominative	*dux*	*ducēs*
Vocative	*dux*	*ducēs*
Accusative	*ducem*	*ducēs*
Genitive	*ducis*	*ducum*
Dative	*ducī*	*ducibus*
Ablative	*duce*	*ducibus*

4. *comes, comitis,* c. = companion

	Singular	Plural
Nominative	*comes*	*comitēs*
Vocative	*comes*	*comitēs*
Accusative	*comitem*	*comitēs*
Genitive	*comitis*	*comitum*
Dative	*comitī*	*comitibus*
Ablative	*comite*	*comitibus*

5. *coniūnx, coniugis,* c. = wife/husband

	Singular	Plural
Nominative	*coniūnx*	*coniugēs*
Vocative	*coniūnx*	*coniugēs*
Accusative	*coniugem*	*coniugēs*
Genitive	*coniugis*	*coniugum*
Dative	*coniugī*	*coniugibus*
Ablative	*coniuge*	*coniugibus*

6. *clāmor, clāmōris,* m. = shout

	Singular	Plural
Nominative	*clāmor*	*clāmōrēs*
Vocative	*clāmor*	*clāmōrēs*
Accusative	*clāmōrem*	*clāmōrēs*
Genitive	*clāmōris*	*clāmōrum*
Dative	*clāmōrī*	*clāmōribus*
Ablative	*clāmōre*	*clāmōribus*

Exercise 1.2
Translate into Latin

1. *rēgis*
2. *ducum*
3. *comitem*
4. *cum coniuge/uxōre*
5. *cum coniuge*
6. *rēgibus*
7. *in lūce*
8. *in lūcem*
9. *(ō) ducēs*
10. *comitum*
11. *uxōrum/coniugum*
12. *cum ducibus*
13. *vōcem*
14. *senis*
15. *(ō) comitēs*
16. *(ō) comes*
17. *ad lūcem*
18. *ex lūce*
19. *(ō) rēx*
20. *(ō) rēgēs*

Exercise 1.3

1.   *uxor, uxōris*, f. = wife
2.   *virtūs, virtūtis*, f. = courage, manly virtue
3.   *homō, hominis*, c. = human being, man/woman
4.   *comes, comitis*, c. = companion
5.   *clāmor, clāmōris*, m. = shout
6.   *mīles, mīlitis*, c. = soldier
7.   *senex, senis*, m. = old man
8.   *lūx, lūcis*, f. = light

Exercise 1.4

1.   *mīlitis*
2.   *hominis*
3.   *senum*
4.   *mulierēs*
5.   *uxōrēs/coniugēs*
6.   *iuvenī*
7.   *iuvenibus*
8.   *mīlitēs!*
9.   *virtūte*
10. *cum uxōribus/coniugibus*
11. *mīlitum*
12. *hominum*
13. *senis*
14. *mulierem*
15. *uxor/coniūnx*
16. *ad iuvenem*
17. *ad iuvenēs*
18. *mīles!*
19. *senēs!*
20. *senex!*

Exercise 1.5

1.   The leader led (his) soldiers into battle.
2.   Kings are often old men.
3.   Laelia's husband was a young man.
4.   There is no light in the temple.
5.   Are you the king's companions?
6.   I heard a shout.
7.   The men are standing in the street.
8.   Good leaders have courage.
9.   We praise the courage of young men.
10. The old man does not have a wife.

Exercise 1.6

1.   *Quīntus, poēta, rēgem laudat.*
2.   *iuvenēs senī auxilium dedērunt.*
3.   *ubi est mulieris coniūnx?*
4.   *nautae cum mīlitibus pugnābant.*
5.   *uxor cārum coniugem amāvit.*
6.   *iuvenēs mīlitēs esse cupiunt.*
7.   *in caelō lūx est.*
8.   *puellae mulieris comitēs erant.*
9.   *rēx mīlitis virtūtem laudāvit.*
10. *vōcem ducis nōn audīvimus.*

Exercise 1.7

1.   (a)   He possessed many sheep and a son.
     (b)   No, he was a young man.
     (c)   He must look after the sheep.
     (d)   No; he is silly and timid and very much afraid of wolves.
     (e)   No, many shepherds lived near him.
     (f)   They wanted to eat the sheep.
     (g)   Loudly.
     (h)   The arrival of many shepherds with spears.

2.   There was a shepherd, who had many sheep; he also had a son. Once upon a time, when the son was already a young man, the father went away; and he said to his son: 'I am going away now, and you must look after the sheep.' The shepherd's son was silly and timid; he was very much afraid of wolves. Many shepherds lived near our shepherd; and when wolves wanted to come into a stable and eat the sheep, the master of the stable used to shout loudly 'Wolves are here! Wolves!' Then many shepherds would hurry into the stable with spears; and the wolves used to flee, terrified.

3.   (a)   Acc. pl.
       (b)   Dat. sing.
       (c)   *dīxērunt*
       (d)   *discēdēbam*
       (e)   *pāstōrum fīliī*
       (f)   Present infinitive of *veniō*: to come
       (g)   *prope (nostrum) pastōrem* (line 5) = near (our) shepherd
             īn stabulum (line 6) = into the stable
             cum hastīs (lines 8-9)= with spears
             īn stabulum (line 9) = into the stable
       (h)   *absunt*

Exercise 1.8

1.   1st person singular   *laudābō*   I shall praise
      2nd person singular   *laudābis*   you (singular) will praise
      3rd person singular   *laudābit*   he, she or it will praise
      1st person plural   *laudābimus*   we shall praise
      2nd person plural   *laudābitis*   you (plural) will praise
      3rd person plural   *laudābunt*   they will praise

2.   1st person singular   *nāvigābō*   I shall sail
      2nd person singular   *nāvigābis*   you (singular) will sail
      3rd person singular   *nāvigābit*   he, she or it will sail
      1st person plural   *nāvigābimus*   we shall sail
      2nd person plural   *nāvigābitis*   you (plural) will sail
      3rd person plural   *nāvigābunt*   they will sail

3.   1st person singular   *rogābō*   I shall ask
      2nd person singular   *rogābis*   you (singular) will ask
      3rd person singular   *rogābit*   he, she or it will ask
      1st person plural   *rogābimus*   we shall ask
      2nd person plural   *rogābitis*   you (plural) will ask
      3rd person plural   *rogābunt*   they will ask

4.   1st person singular   *festīnābō*   I shall hurry
      2nd person singular   *festīnābis*   you (singular) will hurry
      3rd person singular   *festīnābit*   he, she or it will hurry
      1st person plural   *festīnābimus*   we shall hurry
      2nd person plural   *festīnābitis*   you (plural) will hurry
      3rd person plural   *festīnābunt*   they will hurry

5.	1st person singular	*spectābō*	I shall watch
	2nd person singular	*spectābis*	you (singular) will watch
	3rd person singular	*spectābit*	he, she or it will watch
	1st person plural	*spectābimus*	we shall watch
	2nd person plural	*spectābitis*	you (plural) will watch
	3rd person plural	*spectābunt*	they will watch

6.	1st person singular	*vocābō*	I shall call
	2nd person singular	*vocābis*	you (singular) will call
	3rd person singular	*vocābit*	he, she or it will call
	1st person plural	*vocābimus*	we shall call
	2nd person plural	*vocābitis*	you (plural) will call
	3rd person plural	*vocābunt*	they will call

Exercise 1.9

1.	He will praise	11.	You (pl.) will build
2.	We shall sail	12.	They will live/inhabit
3.	They will ask	13.	He will work
4.	He will hurry	14.	I shall attack
5.	You (sing.) will watch	15.	We shall kill
6.	I shall praise	16.	They will carry
7.	I sail	17.	They fight
8.	You (pl.) will ask	18.	You (pl.) will watch
9.	We hurry	19.	I shall overcome
10.	We shall watch	20.	He will call

Exercise 1.10

1.	*laudābit.*	11.	*nautae pugnābunt.*
2.	*festīnābunt.*	12.	*puellae cantābunt.*
3.	*spectābō.*	13.	*dominī festīnābunt.*
4.	*laudābitis.*	14.	*poētās laudābunt.*
5.	*amābunt.*	15.	*agricolās spectābimus.*
6.	*cantābimus.*	16.	*dī oppidum oppugnābunt.*
7.	*pugnābit.*	17.	*Rōmulus mūrum aedificābit.*
8.	*nāvigābunt.*	18.	*Rōmulus Remum necābit.*
9.	*rogābō.*	19.	*Rōmulus Remum necat.*
10.	*nōn pugnābis.*	20.	*Rōmulus Remum necāvit.*

Exercise 1.11

1.	1st person singular	*dēlēbō*	I shall destroy
	2nd person singular	*dēlēbis*	you (singular) will destroy
	3rd person singular	*dēlēbit*	he, she or it will destroy
	1st person plural	*dēlēbimus*	we shall destroy
	2nd person plural	*dēlēbitis*	you (plural) will destroy
	3rd person plural	*dēlēbunt*	they will destroy

2.
1st person singular	*rīdēbō*	I shall laugh
2nd person singular	*rīdēbis*	you (singular) will laugh
3rd person singular	*rīdēbit*	he, she or it will laugh
1st person plural	*rīdēbimus*	we shall laugh
2nd person plural	*rīdēbitis*	you (plural) will laugh
3rd person plural	*rīdēbunt*	they will laugh

3.
1st person singular	*habēbō*	I shall have
2nd person singular	*habēbis*	you (singular) will have
3rd person singular	*habēbit*	he, she or it will have
1st person plural	*habēbimus*	we shall have
2nd person plural	*habēbitis*	you (plural) will have
3rd person plural	*habēbunt*	they will have

4.
1st person singular	*iubēbō*	I shall order
2nd person singular	*iubēbis*	you (singular) will order
3rd person singular	*iubēbit*	he, she or it will order
1st person plural	*iubēbimus*	we shall order
2nd person plural	*iubēbitis*	you (plural) will order
3rd person plural	*iubēbunt*	they will order

5.
1st person singular	*respondēbō*	I shall reply
2nd person singular	*respondēbis*	you (singular) will reply
3rd person singular	*respondēbit*	he, she or it will reply
1st person plural	*respondēbimus*	we shall reply
2nd person plural	*respondēbitis*	you (plural) will reply
3rd person plural	*respondēbunt*	they will reply

6.
1st person singular	*vidēbō*	I shall see
2nd person singular	*vidēbis*	you (singular) will see
3rd person singular	*vidēbit*	he, she or it will see
1st person plural	*vidēbimus*	we shall see
2nd person plural	*vidēbitis*	you (plural) will see
3rd person plural	*vidēbunt*	they will see

Exercise 1.12

1. They will destroy
2. You (sing.) will order
3. He will terrify
4. I shall have
5. You (pl.) will order
6. Will they terrify?
7. They will reply
8. We shall hold
9. He will order
10. I shall see
11. They will warn
12. You (sing.) will have
13. I shall reply
14. They hold
15. They were ordering
16. You (sing.) were seeing
17. They will watch
18. You (pl.) will destroy
19. We shall laugh
20. They will have

Exercise 1.13

1. *habēbunt.*
2. *monēbō.*
3. *tenēbit.*
4. *respondēbimus.*
5. *terrēbunt.*
6. *habēbit.*
7. *rīdēbimus.*
8. *vidēbitis.*
9. *tenēbō.*
10. *nōn terrēbunt.*
11. *timēbuntne?*
12. *nōn respondēbō.*
13. *habēbis.*
14. *nōn habēbis.*
15. *timēbimus.*
16. *tenēbis.*
17. *iubēbant.*
18. *nōn monēbimus.*
19. *habēbit.*
20. *nōn videō.*

Exercise 1.14

1. Tomorrow I shall hurry with (my) companions to the fields.
2. Afterwards the soldiers will attack the town.
3. We shall praise the king and queen.
4. The leader will order the soldiers to fight.
5. Soon the boys will shout, but the girls will sing.
6. Will the young men terrify us with shouts?
7. The frightened boys will not reply to the master.
8. The mothers will prepare the food for (their) sons. (Bonus mark: dat. pl. of *filius* = *filiīs*; dat. pl. of *filia* = *filiābus*)
9. Today the king will give gold to the poets.
10. Tomorrow the girl will see (her) mother.

From now on, the use of the possessive will not be bracketed (see note below Exercise 1.15 on page 12 of the pupil's book).

Exercise 1.15

1. *patrēs fīliōs librōs legere iubēbunt.*
2. *sorōrem amābit.*
3. *hodiē incolae in oppidō manēbunt.*
4. *mīlitēs ducem laudābunt.*
5. *mox nautae ad īnsulam nāvigābunt.*
6. *crās iuvenēs in agrīs rīdēbunt.*
7. *hominēs dē mīlitibus monēbō.*
8. *ex oppidō celeriter festīnābitis.*
9. *clāmōrēs iuvenum nōn timēbimus.*
10. *terrēbuntne mulierēs īrātī senēs?*

Exercise 1.16

1. *virtus* + (d) virtue: *virtus* = courage; courage is a type of manly virtue.
2. *iuvenis* + (g) juvenile: *iuvenis* = young man; juvenile means immature.
3. *rēx* + (f) regal: *rēx* = king; regal means kingly.
4. *mīles* + (b) military: *mīles* = soldier; military means to do with soldiers.
5. *frāter* + (c) fraternal: *frāter* = brother; fraternal means brotherly or of a brother.
6. *senex* + (e) senile: *senex* = old man; if someone is senile, he is suffering from the effects of old age.
7. *pater* + (h) paternal: *pater* = father; paternal means fatherly or of a father.
8. *vōx* + (a) vocal: *vōx* = voice; vocal means of the voice (e.g. vocal chords).

Exercise 1.17

1. *flūmen, flūminis,* n. = river

	Singular	**Plural**
Nominative	*flūmen*	*flūmina*
Vocative	*flūmen*	*flūmina*
Accusative	*flūmen*	*flūmina*
Genitive	*flūminis*	*flūminum*
Dative	*flūminī*	*flūminibus*
Ablative	*flūmine*	*flūminibus*

2. *iter, itineris,* n. = journey

	Singular	**Plural**
Nominative	*iter*	*itinera*
Vocative	*iter*	*itinera*
Accusative	*iter*	*itinera*
Genitive	*itineris*	*itinerum*
Dative	*itinerī*	*itineribus*
Ablative	*itinere*	*itineribus*

Exercise 1.18

1. Then the boy, called Marcus, walked to the river.
2. The sailors will sail to the island tomorrow.
3. Today I decided to make a journey.
4. Who does not have a name?
5. I shall always love rivers and fields.
6. We shall warn the kings about the leaders.
7. The leader's companions made journeys.
8. The master was calling his wife.
9. Yesterday we saw our mother.
10. Afterwards we shall hurry quickly into the town.

Exercise 1.19

1. *rēgīna ancillās amat.*
2. *magistrī parvōs puerōs laudābant.*
3. *puellae bonae servōs vocābant.*
4. *magistrōs saevōs nōn amāmus.*
5. *nautae malī multōs incolās necant.*
6. *ducēs rēgis fortiter pugnābunt.*
7. *per flūmina nāvigābimus.*
8. *quis ducī respondēbit?*
9. *saepe senēs itinera faciēbant.*
10. *iuvenēs multōs comitēs habēbunt.*

Exercise 1.20

1. (a) Because he kept watching the fields.
   (b) He heard a savage wind.
   (c) They were sleeping.
   (d) They ran quickly to the young man's stable.
   (e) *aberat* = it was absent.
   (f) *tandem* = at last.
   (g) *sōlus* = alone.
   (h) He kept watching the fields again.

2. The shepherd's son did not sleep by night, but always kept watching the fields. Suddenly he heard a savage wind. 'There's a wolf here!' he shouted, 'a wolf,' and he called the shepherds loudly. The shepherds were sleeping, but when they heard the young man's shout, they ran quickly to the young man's stable. They investigated the whole stable, but there was no wolf. At last the shepherds went away, and the shepherd's son was alone again and kept watching the fields.

3. (a) *dormit.*
   (b) *agrum.*
   (c) *spectābit.*
   (d) *ventōs saevōs.*
   (e) *adsunt.*
   (f) Perfect (past) tense; *clāmāvērunt* and *vocāvērunt.*
   (g) *iuvenī, iuvenibus.*
   (h) *currō.*

Chapter 2

Exercise 2.1

1. Tell me the names of the strong boys.
2. What did the soldier report to you?
3. I shall warn the leader about you.
4. The girls were singing clear words to me.
5. Your wife will give you help.
6. Why did you warn the king about me?
7. Laelia said many words to me.
8. Marcus will hurry to you.
9. Quintus wrote about the rivers.
10. I shall order you to remain in the town.

Exercise 2.2

1. *dē mē cantābit.*
2. *magistrum, Quīnte, dē tē monēbimus.*
3. *nōmen tibi puerī dīxērunt.*
4. *ō rēx, puerī tibi librum magnum dabunt.*
5. *tū Laelia hīc manēbis, sed ego templum intrābō.*
6. *māter, tē mox vocābimus.*
7. *dīxit servus 'dā mihi dominum bonum'.*
8. *domine, cibumne tibi parābō?*
9. *verba mihi multa scrībe, Aule.*
10. *Mārcus ad mē crās festīnābit.*

Exercise 2.3

1. *rēgem bonum* = the good king
2. *rēgēs bonī* = the good kings
3. *ducis bonī* = the good leader
4. *comitum bonōrum* = of the good companions
5. *cum mīlitibus bonīs* = with the good soldiers
6. *coniūnx bona* = the good wife
7. *hominem bonum* = the good man
8. *clāmōrī bonō* = to the good shout
9. *rēgum bonōrum* = of the good kings
10. *cum iuvene bonō* = with the good youth
11. *comitēs bonī* = good companions
12. *comitēs bonōs* = good companions
13. *vōx bona* = good voice
14. *lūcem bonam* = good light
15. *senem bonum* = the good old man
16. *virtūtem bonam* = good courage
17. *mulierum bonārum* = of good women
18. *uxōrum bonārum* = of the good wives
19. *mātrēs bonae* = oh, good mothers
20. *sorōrī bonae* = to the good sister

Exercise 2.4

1. The good leaders.
2. The beautiful women.
3. To the small brother.
4. To the savage men.
5. The friends of kings are often tired old men.
6. The boys will stand in bright light.
7. You and I played in the field.
8. The happy brothers praised their companions' courage.
9. Bad sons have an angry father.
10. Good sons are dear to their happy father.

Exercise 2.5

1. Good leaders lead good soldiers.
2. Beautiful women live in the town.
3. The small girls have a strong brother.
4. The inhabitants feared the savage young men.
5. You will praise the great courage of the soldiers.
6. The old men feared the bright light.
7. The wicked son of the king terrified the inhabitants.
8. The strong soldiers defended their fatherland.
9. Oh, strong leader, why do you not attack the small town?
10. You and I have a beautiful mother.

Exercise 2.6

1. *mīlitēs malī ducem bonum timēbunt.*
2. *rēgem habēre validum cupimus.*
3. *mulierēs miserae ducem saevum timent.*
4. *frātrēs nōtī sorōrem pulchram habent.*
5. *laetī sunt servī rēgis laetī.*
6. *turbam habēbit multōrum comitum.*
7. *ego et tū, Mārce, ducēs magnōs vidēbimus.*
8. *puerī per flūmen altum nāvigābunt.*
9. *iuvenēs miserōs senēs nōn timēbunt.*
10. *terrēbitne coniūnx īrātus uxōrem pulchram?*

Exercise 2.7

1. There are many islands in the sea.
2. Big men have big bodies.
3. I love rivers, but my friend loves the sea.
4. I greatly fear seas, because they are big.
5. Soldiers used to have and to give many wounds in battles.
6. Old men's bodies are often tired.
7. 'Where is our sea?' the small boy asked. 'Tell me.'
8. Many soldiers do not fear wounds.

Exercise 2.8

1. *puerō vulnus dare nōn cupiunt.*
2. *corpora agricolārum valida sunt.*
3. *nautae in marī nāvigābunt.*
4. *trēs mihi hastās et quattuor gladiōs date.*
5. *dīxit Rōmānus 'mare nostrum magnum est et pulchrum.'*
6. *tibi aquam et vīnum dabimus.*
7. *rēx vōcem clāram habet.*
8. *iuvenēs mātribus cārī sunt.*

Exercise 2.9

1.   (a) The moon.
    (b) He thought they were shadows of wolves.
    (c) They investigated the stable again.
    (d) *lupī aberant* = the wolves were absent.
    (e) *mox* = soon.
    (f) *īrātī* = angry.
    (g) They laughed and remained in their beds.
    (h) The wolves ate the sheep and the young man.

2. The young man was watching the fields; suddenly the moon came out (lit. there was a moon) and he saw the shadows of the trees. 'Wolves are here!' he shouted, 'wolves!' and he loudly called the shepherds who were asleep. The shepherds came and again they investigated the stable but the wolves were not there. Soon they went away angry; the young man was alone. Suddenly he saw long shadows and heard savage cries. 'Wolves are here!' he shouted, 'wolves!' and again and again he called the shepherds loudly; but the shepherds laughed and remained in their beds; and the wolves ate the sheep and the young man.

3.   (a) *spectābit.*
    (b) Genitive plural.
    (c) *discessit.*
    (d) *īrātus.*
    (e) Accusative plural.
    (f) *rīdēbunt.*
    (g) *manēbant.*
    (h) *iuvenibus.*

Exercise 2.10

1. They will hurry with me to the town.
2. I want to play with you.
3. Who will sail with us?
4. Bad men were terrifying us.
5. Will you give us swords and spears?
6. 'Tomorrow,' said the master 'I shall walk with you.'
7. The good soldiers will give you help.
8. Many men do not praise me.
9. We are here; you are there.
10. The messenger ran to us.

Exercise 2.11

1. *vōbīscum ad nōs festīnābunt.*
2. *dā nōbīs cibum, domine.*
3. *saevī mīlitēs nōs terrēbunt.*
4. *quis nōbīscum ad rēgem bonum venit?*
5. *equus validus ad vōs currit.*
6. *multī mēcum et tēcum pugnābunt.*
7. *nōs hīc manēbimus; vōs ad agrōs ambulābitis.*
8. *quis nōbīs cibum parābit?*
9. *ducēs bonī vōbīs auxilium dabunt.*
10. *ō Pūblī, nōmen rēgis mihi dīc.*

Exercise 2.12

1. *mare* = sea; maritime means concerned with the sea. (Also: marina, marine.)
2. *corpus* = body; corporal means affecting the body. (Also: corpulent, corpse.)
3. *vulnus* = wound; vulnerable means liable to being wounded. (Also: invulnerable.)
4. *nārrō* = I tell; a narrator tells a story. (Also: narrative, narration, narrate.)
5. *māter* = mother; maternal means belonging or relating to a mother. (Also: maternal.)
6. *nōmen* = name; to nominate is to name. (Also: nominal, nomenclature.)

Exercise 2.13

1. *hoc oppidum* = this town
2. *hanc puellam* = this girl
3. *haec māter* = this mother
4. *huic virō* = to this man
5. *huius magistrī* = of this teacher
6. *huic nautae* = to this sailor
7. *hoc templum* = this temple
8. *hoc vīnum* = this wine
9. *hic agricola* = this farmer
10. *hunc puerum* = this boy

Exercise 2.14

1. Hurry into the town with me and this boy!
2. I shall order this girl to sing.
3. His/her mother is a good woman.
4. I gave a sword to this man.
5. Tell me the name of this master.
6. The sailors have departed from this town.
7. I shall soon see this temple.
8. This wine is strong and good.
9. This farmer will work in the field.
10. This woman loves this man.

Exercise 2.15

1. *in oppidum cum hōc puerō festīnābō.*
2. *huius mulieris fīlia pulchra est.*
3. *huic mīlitī aquam dabis.*
4. *vīdistisne hanc puellam?*
5. *haec bona est; hic quoque bonus est.*
6. *in hāc urbe manēbimus.*
7. *in hoc templum currēbant.*
8. *ab hāc īnsulā nāvigābimus.*
9. *vidēbitisne hunc agrum?*
10. *fīlium huius virī vīdērunt.*

Exercise 2.16

1. (a) Ibycus was a Greek poet.
   (b) He was making a journey.
   (c) They decided to kill him.
   (d) He saw some cranes flying through the sky.
   (e) He prophesied that the cranes would report the crime to the inhabitants of the town.
   (f) The cranes flew suddenly through the sky.
   (g) Very low. It was not very bright to give the show away to the inhabitants of the town.
   (h) *facinus nostrum* = our crime.
   (i) The inhabitants heard the words of the robber and immediately punished him with his friends.

2. There was once a Greek poet called Ibycus; he was making a journey; suddenly wicked men took Ibycus' money and decided to kill him. Suddenly some cranes flew through the sky; and when Ibycus saw the cranes, he said 'The cranes which are flying through the sky will report this crime to the inhabitants of the

town.' Then the wicked men killed the poet and came into the town; and suddenly the cranes flew through the sky. 'Behold!' shouted one of the men to his friends, 'here are the cranes which, as Ibycus said, will report our crime to the inhabitants of the town.' The inhabitants heard his words and immediately punished him with his friends.

3. (a) Ablative singular; by name.
    (b) Accusative singular; it is the object of *faciēbat*.
    (c) *hanc pecūniam*.
    (d) *volābunt*.
    (e) Accusative singular; it is the object of *nūntiābunt*.
    (f) Perfect (past) tense of *veniō:* they came.
    (g) Genitive singular: his.
    (h) *audiunt*.

Exercise 2.17

1. *agricolae nautās monent.*
2. *magister bonus puellās bonās laudābat.*
3. *malī puerī equōs nostrōs terrent.*
4. *incolae fessī viam longam spectābant.*
5. *puellae pulchrae verba bona nūntiābant.*
6. *mīlitēs per oppidum nōbīscum errābunt.*
7. *ducēsne senibus auxilium dabunt?*
8. *frātrī nostrō librōs dabimus.*
9. *hanc urbem mox vidēbitis.*
10. *in templō mēcum cantābit.*

Exercise 2.18

1. *hōs nautās* = these sailors
2. *cum hīs puellīs* = with these girls
3. *haec oppida* = these towns
4. *in hīs agrīs* = in these fields
5. *hī magistrī* = these teachers
6. *haec mulier* = this woman
7. *hī senēs* = these old men
8. *hōrum mīlitum* = of these soldiers
9. *hōrum iuvenum* = of these young men
10. *hīs rēgibus* = to these kings

Exercise 2.19

1. These farmers will overcome these sailors.
2. These boys will not fight with these girls.
3. This town is theirs.
4. Many horses live in these fields; I shall give them food.
5. This master was praising these girls.
6. His mother is a beautiful woman.
7. The old men gave him a book.
8. These things are good.
9. She is good.
10. These waves are savage.

Exercise 2.20

1. *nūntiābitne haec verba dominus?*
2. *hī equī in agrīs stābunt.*
3. *servī hōrum adsunt.*
4. *puerī hās puellās laudāvērunt.*
5. *hae mulierēs hanc urbem habitant.*
6. *bona verba nūntiābat; audīvistisne haec?*
7. *hī librī huius sunt.*
8. *hī librī hōrum sunt.*
9. *hī malī cum hīs incolīs pugnant.*
10. *hōs gladiōs hīs mīlitibus date.*

Chapter 3

Exercise 3.1

1. *clārior* = clearer; *clārissimus* = clearest
2. *saevior* = more savage; *saevissimus* = most savage
3. *cārior* = dearer; *cārissimus* = dearest
4. *nōtior* = better-known; *nōtissimus* = best-known
5. *altior* = higher/deeper; *altissimus* = highest/deepest
6. *īrātior* = angrier; *īrātissimus* = angriest
7. *longior* = longer; *longissimus* = longest
8. *laetior* = happier; *laetissimus* = happiest

Exercise 3.2

1. The voice of a boy is clearer than the voice of an old man.
2. I haven't seen more savage soldiers.
3. A good master is dearer to a girl than a bad one.
4. Who is better-known than this king?
5. Seas are deeper than rivers.
6. The boys were angrier than the girls.
7. This road is longer than ours.
8. Our temple is better-known than yours.

Exercise 3.3

1. *mare nostrum altius est quam vestrum.*
2. *mīlitēs saeviōrēs sunt.*
3. *hic gladius hāc hastā longior est.*
4. *flūmen altum, sed mare altius est.*
5. *quis mihi cārior est quam amīcus meus?*
6. *puerum laetiōrem nōn vīdī.*
7. *senēs īrātiōrēs sunt iuvenibus.*
8. *templum altius est quam hic mūrus.*

Exercise 3.4

1. Who is the best-known of the leaders?
2. Have you seen the very famous woman?
3. On this island this road is the longest.
4. The mother is very dear to her sons and daughters.
5. These old men are the angriest of the inhabitants.
6. This wound is very deep.

Exercise 3.5

1. *quis est nautārum īrātissimus?*
2. *hic puer nōtissimum patrem habet.*
3. *haec mulier clārissima est incolārum.*
4. *hic templum altissimum aedificābit.*
5. *hic mīles saevissimus est.*
6. *hic mihi frātrum cārissimus est.*

Exercise 3.6

1. Where is that girl?
2. This boy is happier than that one.
3. That old man is very angry.
4. Have you seen that woman?
5. Tomorrow we shall hurry into that town.
6. I shall give the book to that woman.
7. Will you fight with that soldier?
8. His father is very well-known.
9. This little sailor is more savage than that big one.
10. The master will praise that boy.

Exercise 3.7

1. *haec puella illā laetior est.*
2. *illum agrum spectāte, mīlitēs.*
3. *in illud oppidum vōbīscum festīnābimus.*
4. *crās illum puerum vidēbō.*
5. *nāvigābitisne, nautae, per illud flūmen?*
6. *Mārce, hunc librum illī magistrō dā!*
7. *illī mulierī herī illum librum dedī.*
8. *estne Quīntus illīus puellae frāter?*
9. *ille agricola Aulī pater est.*
10. *crās cum illō mīlite pugnābō.*

Exercise 3.8

1. (a) Croesus was king of Lydia.
    (b) Solon was a philosopher.
    (c) He showed him much money and gold.
    (d) 'Who is the most fortunate man in the world?'
    (e) He did not say that Croesus was the most fortunate.
    (f) He was very angry.
    (g) Death.
    (h) Because a happy man will not perhaps always be happy.
    (i) Croesus laughed at it.
    (j) He did not praise Solon.

2. Lydia was a great land and it had many inhabitants; it had a king called Croesus. Once upon a time the philosopher Solon made a journey into Lydia. Croesus called him to his palace and showed him much money and much gold; and he asked Solon 'Who is the most fortunate man in the world?' Twice he asked him; but Solon did not reply 'You are.' Therefore the king was very angry and said to Solon 'I am a great king, I rule many people and I have much gold; why did you not say to me "You are the most fortunate of men" ?' Solon replied 'A happy man will perhaps not always be happy; no one therefore is fortunate before he is dead.' Croesus laughed at this and did not praise Solon.

3. (a)   *nōmen* = a name
    (b)   Ablative singular
    (c)   *itinera fēcit*
    (d)   (i) *illam,* (ii) no change
    (e)   Ablative singular, because it follows *in* = 'in' (rather than 'into')
    (f)   *respondērunt*
    (g)   *dīcēbat*
    (h)   Dative singular
    (i)   *tibi*
    (j)   It is generally not written first word in a sentence

Exercise 3.9

1.   *illī mīlitēs* = those soldiers.
2.   *illōs ducēs* = those leaders.
3.   *illōrum librōrum* = of those books.
4.   *in illō templō* = in that temple.
5.   *illīs mulieribus* = to those women.
6.   *illōs incolās* = those inhabitants.
7.   *illōrum comitum* = of those companions.
8.   *illīus equī* = of that horse.
9.   *ille rēx* = that king.
10. *illae mātrēs* = those mothers.

Exercise 3.10

1.   Those soldiers are strong; the rest however are not.
2.   Those few leaders do not want to wage war.
3.   Give these few books to those girls!
4.   The rest of the women were absent.
5.   Who has stood in the middle of the road with those boys?
6.   A few soldiers were freeing those inhabitants.
7.   Did those men punish the rest of the boys?
8.   Those horses are in the middle of the field.
9.   The good king will free those slaves and save them.
10. Why is the mother of those girls absent?

Exercise 3.11

1.   *quis cēterās hastās illīs mīlitibus dabit?*
2.   *illās paucās mulierēs līberāvī.*
3.   *illī magistrī cēterōs puerōs nōn pūnīvērunt.*
4.   *ubi sunt illārum puellārum librī?*
5.   *agricolae bonī illōs paucōs equōs līberābunt.*
6.   *illōs magistrōs in mediā urbe salūtābimus.*
7.   *cūr illī cēterōs incolās pūniēbant?*
8.   *Sextus et Aulus illōs paucōs nautās salūtābunt.*
9.   *illī in mediā viā stābant.*
10. *hodiē paucī poētae in templō sunt.*

Exercise 3.12

1.   The boy was playing in the field alone.
2.   This spear belongs to (lit. is of) Marcus alone.
3.   He has one sword and one spear.
4.   Announce those words to the king alone.
5.   I have given these gifts to one boy.
6.   That girl will sing alone in the temple.
7.   I shall hurry into the town with one man.
8.   In that land there is only (lit. alone) one river.

Exercise 3.13

1.   *rēx sōlus pugnābat.*
2.   *rēgīna sōla laeta fuit.*
3.   *pater est ūnīus sōlīus puellae.*
4.   *illī magistrō sōlī librōs dedimus.*
5.   *cum illō ūnō mīlite pugnābāmus.*
6.   *Laelia et Sulpicia illa dōna ūnī mulierī dedērunt.*
7.   *quis sōlus in templō manēbit?*
8.   *ūnus puer circum templum illum mūrum aedificāvit.*

Exercise 3.14

1.   *regēmus*
2.   *dūcam*
3.   *vincet*
4.   *legēs*
5.   *mittent*
6.   *scrībēmus*
7.   *ostendam*
8.   *pugnābit*
9.   *stābitis*
10. *lūdent*

Exercise 3.15

1.	1st person singular	*dīcam*
	2nd person singular	*dīcēs*
	3rd person singular	*dīcet*
	1st person plural	*dīcēmus*
	2nd person plural	*dīcētis*
	3rd person plural	*dīcent*

2.	1st person singular	*faciam*
	2nd person singular	*faciēs*
	3rd person singular	*faciet*
	1st person plural	*faciēmus*
	2nd person plural	*faciētis*
	3rd person plural	*facient*

3.	1st person singular	*veniam*
	2nd person singular	*veniēs*
	3rd person singular	*veniet*
	1st person plural	*veniēmus*
	2nd person plural	*veniētis*
	3rd person plural	*venient*

4.	1st person singular	*bibam*
	2nd person singular	*bibēs*
	3rd person singular	*bibet*
	1st person plural	*bibēmus*
	2nd person plural	*bibētis*
	3rd person plural	*bibent*

5.	1st person singular	*iaciam*
	2nd person singular	*iaciēs*
	3rd person singular	*iaciet*
	1st person plural	*iaciēmus*
	2nd person plural	*iaciētis*
	3rd person plural	*iacient*

6.	1st person singular	*dormiam*
	2nd person singular	*dormiēs*
	3rd person singular	*dormiet*
	1st person plural	*dormiēmus*
	2nd person plural	*dormiētis*
	3rd person plural	*dormient*

Exercise 3.16

1. The leader will lead his soldiers into battle.
2. Tomorrow we shall sleep in the town.
3. Will you soon wage war?
4. Afterwards we shall eat food.
5. The farmers will run to the river.
6. Claudia and Sulpicia will depart from the island.
7. Titus will play with Publius in the field.
8. Will you write a new book, Quintus?
9. This king will conquer that king.
10. I shall now read this book.

Exercise 3.17

1. *quis hanc terram reget?*
2. *hī puerī hunc cibum nōn cōnsūment.*
3. *crās iter faciam.*
4. *in mare ruētis.*
5. *vincentne illōs mīlitēs?*
6. *in templum trēs librōs portābis.*
7. *nautae illud aurum capere nōn cupient.*
8. *verba ducis audiēmus.*
9. *quid illīs saevīs mīlitibus dīcent?*
10. *semperne illae mulierēs illōs senēs amābunt?*

Exercise 3.18

1. *puerī mūrum altum aedificant.*
2. *magistrī bonās puellās laudant.*
3. *malōs nautās superāmus.*
4. *dominī servōs monēbant.*
5. *illōs magnōs equōs spectābās.*
6. *quis hōs incolās regere cupiet?*
7. *hae mulierēs clārissimae sunt.*
8. *illī mīlitēs saevissimī erant.*
9. *Sextus et Gnaeus cum Cassiā nōn pugnābunt.*
10. *Quīntus, poēta, multōs librōs scrīpsit.*

Exercise 3.19

1. Median; *medius* = middle. The median of a set of numbers is the middle number. (Also: medium.)
2. Solo; *sōlus* = alone. A solo performance is when one performs on one's own. (Also: sole, solitary.)
3. Punitive; *pūniō* = I punish. If one takes punitive steps against someone, one punishes them. (Also: punish, punishment.)
4. Liberate; *līberō* = I set free. To liberate is to set free. (Also: liberation.)
5. Conserve; *servō* = I save. To conserve is to keep safe or protect. (Also: conservation, preserve.)

Exercise 3.20

1. (a) Because Cyrus was always getting stronger and stronger
    (b) He sent messengers to Delphi
    (c) To ask the priestess whether he should go to war with Cyrus
    (d) Through her, the god advised men about the future
    (e) The waging of a war with Cyrus
    (f) Misleading
    (g) Because he thought he would destroy the empire of Cyrus
    (h) His own

2. Cyrus was king of the Persians; he was always (getting) stronger and stronger; Croesus wanted to wage war with him. Therefore he sent messengers to Delphi*; for the very sacred oracle of the god Apollo was there; a very famous priestess used to inhabit it; through her the god advised men about the future; and men believed this priestess. Therefore the messengers of Croesus asked her 'Ought Croesus to wage war with Cyrus?' She replied '(By doing) so he will destroy a great empire.' When Croesus heard this, he was happy and waged war, but Cyrus defeated Croesus; and Croesus understood the words of the priestess; for he did destroy a great empire: he did not, however, destroy Cyrus' empire, as he expected, but his own.

* N.B. This may be a good time to teach pupils that when going 'to' or 'from' towns or small islands, a preposition is not used.

3. (a) The comparative (nominative, masculine singular).
    (b) *validissimus*.
    (c) *gerō, gerere, gessī, gestum* = I carry on, wage (a war).
    (d) *cupiō, cupere, cupīvī, cupītum* = I desire.
    (e) Feminine, dative singular.
    (f) *rogāvit*.
    (g) *vincēbat*.
    (h) *dēlēvērunt*.

Chapter 4

Exercise 4.1

1.
1st person singular	*festīnāveram*	I had hurried
2nd person singular	*festīnāverās*	you (sing.) had hurried
3rd person singular	*festīnāverat*	he, she, it had hurried
1st person plural	*festīnāverāmus*	we had hurried
2nd person plural	*festīnāverātis*	you (plur.) had hurried
3rd person plural	*festīnāverant*	they had hurried

2.
1st person singular	*līberāveram*	I had set free
2nd person singular	*līberāverās*	you (sing.) had set free
3rd person singular	*līberāverat*	he, she, it had set free
1st person plural	*līberāverāmus*	we had set free
2nd person plural	*līberāverātis*	you (plur.) had set free
3rd person plural	*līberāverant*	they had set free

3.
1st person singular	*dēlēveram*	I had destroyed
2nd person singular	*dēlēverās*	you (sing.) had destroyed
3rd person singular	*dēlēverat*	he, she, it had destroyed
1st person plural	*dēlēverāmus*	we had destroyed
2nd person plural	*dēlēverātis*	you (plur.) had destroyed
3rd person plural	*dēlēverant*	they had destroyed

4.
1st person singular	*vīderam*	I had seen
2nd person singular	*vīderās*	you (sing.) had seen
3rd person singular	*vīderat*	he, she, it had seen
1st person plural	*vīderāmus*	we had seen
2nd person plural	*vīderātis*	you (plur.) had seen
3rd person plural	*vīderant*	they had seen

5.
1st person singular	*dormīveram*	I had slept
2nd person singular	*dormīverās*	you (sing.) had slept
3rd person singular	*dormīverat*	he, she, it had slept
1st person plural	*dormīverāmus*	we had slept
2nd person plural	*dormīverātis*	you (plur.) had slept
3rd person plural	*dormīverant*	they had slept

6.
1st person singular	*fēceram*	I had made/done
2nd person singular	*fēcerās*	you (sing.) had made/done
3rd person singular	*fēcerat*	he, she, it had made/done
1st person plural	*fēcerāmus*	we had made/done
2nd person plural	*fēcerātis*	you (plur.) had made/done
3rd person plural	*fēcerant*	they had made/done

Exercise 4.2

1. He had ruled
2. We had taken
3. They had warned
4. He had fallen
5. I had read/chosen
6. You had laughed
7. He had played
8. I had lived, inhabited
9. They had ordered
10. We had shown

Exercise 4.3

1. *monuerat*
2. *rēxerāmus*
3. *audīverant*
4. *cēperās*
5. *dīxerat*
6. *iusserāmus*
7. *lūserātis*
8. *oppugnāverant*
9. *cucurrerāmus*
10. *dederam*

Exercise 4.4

1. When we came into the town, Gnaeus had already left for Rome.
2. I gave a book to the girl, but she had already read it.
3. The teacher praised the boys; they had sung well in the temple.
4. The slaves were happy; for the master had set them free.
5. These (soldiers) conquered those soldiers; a good leader had led these.
6. Those men were tired; they had made a very long journey.
7. Quintus, the poet, was writing his sixth book; he had already written five books.
8. Why did you say bad words to us? We had already often heard them.

Exercise 4.5

1. *servī miserī erant; nam dominus hōs nōn laudāverat.*
2. *ducēs mīlitibus dōna dedērunt; incolās oppidī vīcerant.*
3. *nautās salūtāvimus; ad īnsulam nāvigāverant.*
4. *parvī puerī fessī erant; nam in templum cucurrerant.*
5. *rēx, servī, īrātissimus erat; nam in agrīs nōn labōrāverātis.*
6. *laetissimī erāmus; nam amīcum vīderāmus.*
7. *cūr, Claudia, cibum nōbīscum nōn cōnsūmpsistī? illum tibi parāverāmus.*
8. *in oppidum herī vēnimus; nam festīnāverāmus.*

Exercise 4.6.

1. *pulchrior, pulcherrimus*
2. *clārior, clārissimus*
3. *miserior, miserrimus*
4. *longior, longissimus*
5. *laetior, laetissimus*

Exercise 4.7

1. Sulpicia is a very beautiful woman.
2. Who is more beautiful than I (am)?
3. I saw in the street some very wretched boys.
4. This temple is very sacred.
5. Give this gift to the most beautiful girl.
6. Who is more wretched than that man?
7. That man is the most wretched of the inhabitants.
8. Have you seen more wretched girls?

Exercise 4.8

1. *hae mulierēs pulchriōrēs sunt quam illae.*
2. *ubi sunt miseriōrum puellārum librī?*
3. *quid pulchrius est hōc dōnō?*
4. *hoc templum in locō sacerrimō stat.*
5. *hī puerī miseriōrēs sunt illīs.*
6. *ō Mārce, hunc cibum miseriōrī senī dā.*
7. *Laelia incolārum pulcherrima est.*
8. *multōs librōs fīliae pulchriōrī dant.*

Exercise 4.9

1.
   (a) He ordered his soldiers to throw Croesus into chains.
   (b) He ordered them to build a big pile of firewood and to put Croesus on it.
   (c) He had decided to burn Croesus.
   (d) Croesus cried out Solon's name three times.
   (e) He asked 'Who is Solon and why do you call him?'
   (f) He said that he was a Greek philosopher.
   (g) 'No one is fortunate before he is dead.'
   (h) From then on Cyrus considered Croesus as a companion and friend.

2. When Cyrus saw Croesus he ordered his soldiers to throw him into chains; and he ordered them to build a big pile of firewood and to put Croesus on it (lit. there); for he had decided to burn him. Suddenly Croesus shouted 'Oh, Solon' three times; Cyrus asked 'Who is that Solon? And why do you call him?' Croesus replied 'Solon is a Greek philosopher.' And Croesus told Cyrus Solon's words: 'No one is fortunate before he is dead.' And Cyrus immediately set Croesus free; and afterwards he always had him as a companion and a friend.

3.
   (a) Accusative plural.
   (b) Present infinitive: *iacere* = to throw (line 2); *aedificāre* = to build (line 2); *pōnere* = to place (line 3); *incendere* = to burn (line 3).
   (c) *iusserat.*
   (d) Vocative singular.
   (e) Nominative singular.
   (f) *dīcet.*
   (g) Dative singular.
   (h) 3rd person singular, imperfect tense of *habeō* = I have.

Exercise 4.10

1. This woman will be tired.
2. This boy will be a very well-known man.
3. These soldiers will be dear to their leader.
4. The rest of the men will be angry.
5. The girls will be frightened.
6. Will you be the happiest of the boys?
7. The masters will not be savage.
8. Tomorrow you will not be in the field.
9. Who will be my friend?
10. Soon you will be in the temple with me.

Exercise 4.11

1. *quis perterritus erit?*
2. *hoc flūmen altissimum erit.*
3. *īrātissimī erimus.*
4. *crās in oppidō eritis.*
5. *erisne in templō nōbīscum?*
6. *vulnera mīlitum magna nōn erunt.*
7. *illī senēs fessī erunt.*
8. *hae puellae mulierēs pulchrae erunt.*
9. *mox in īnsulā erō.*
10. *cēterī mīlitēs tūtī erunt.*

Exercise 4.12

1. *hostis, hostium.*
2. *rēgis, rēgum.*
3. *urbis, urbium.*
4. *montis, montium.*
5. *mīlitis, mīlitum.*
6. *partis, partium.*
7. *ducis, ducum.*
8. *mātris, mātrum.*
9. *patris, patrum.*
10. *mulieris, mulierum.*

Exercise 4.13

1. The Romans have conquered their enemy.
2. The king used not to love the leaders of the citizens.
3. Is Rome the most beautiful of cities?
4. This mountain is the highest of the mountains.
5. The soldiers of the enemy were many.
6. This part of the city is more beautiful than that.
7. That girl is very dear to her parents.
8. What did Solon say about death?
9. The enemy will wage war with us.
10. These men are the leaders of the ships.

Exercise 4.14

1. *incolae in urbem novam festīnābunt.*
2. *illa pars montium altissima est.*
3. *hostēs oppidum mox oppugnābunt.*
4. *hī mīlitēs mortem nōn timent.*
5. *ubi sunt senum gladiī?*
6. *timēbitne hic puer cīvium īram?*
7. *illōrum agricolārum corpora validissima sunt.*
8. *ducēs hostium clārissimī sunt.*
9. *hic iuvenis amīcus est frātrum meōrum.*
10. *estne Rōma urbium clārissima?*

Exercise 4.15

1. *cīvis* + (d) civilian: a civilian is a (non-military) member of a city; *cīvis* = citizen.
2. *mōns* + (e) mountain: *mōns* = mountain.
3. *mors* + (c) mortal: mortal means liable to die; *mors* = death.
4. *nāvis* + (f) naval: naval means to do with ships and the navy; *nāvis* = ship.
5. *urbs* + (a) urban: urban means to do with cities; *urbs* = city.
6. *hostēs* + (b) hostile: hostile means opposed to one, especially in war; *hostēs* = enemy.

Exercise 4.16

1. (a) Because he was the most beautiful of the youths.
   (b) He did not want any of them as his friend; he did not praise any of them; and he never played with them.
   (c) No, because Narcissus never played with any of the boys and girls.
   (d) The fact that the water was very clear allowed Narcissus to see his reflection in it.
   (e) Because he had decided to drink.
   (f) No; he is not seeing a face, but rather the reflection of his own face.
   (g) He wanted to become friends with the youth.
   (h) He waved to him.

2. There was a young man called Narcissus; he was the most beautiful of youths; many girls and many boys wanted to have him as their friend; but he did not want to have any of them as his friend. He praised no one; he never played with the boys and girls. Once, when he was alone in the wood, he saw a very clear spring and, because he decided to drink, he approached the spring; and when he looked at the water, he saw there the face of a very beautiful young man and immediately he very much wanted to be the friend of that young man; and he waved at him (lit. greeted him with his arms), and he (the young man) greeted Narcissus; and

Narcissus said to the young man 'I am Narcissus; who are you?' But the young man did not reply.

3.   (a)   Ablative singular of *nōmen, nōminis*, n. = a name. Called (by name).
       (b)   This is the genitive plural. Being a non-increasing 3rd declension noun, we would have expected a genitive plural in '*-ium*'; but *iuvenis* joins a number of 'family' nouns in forming its genitive plural in '*-um*'.
       (c)   *cupiēbant*.
       (d)   *cum puerō et puellā*.
       (e)   *lūdō, lūdere, lūsī, lūsum* = I play.
       (f)   *vīderat*.
       (g)   *illud* and *illud*.
       (h)   *mēcum*.

Exercise 4.17

1. *fēminae incolās malōs monēbant.*
2. *magistrī īrātī puerōs fessōs nōn laudant.*
3. *rēgīna ancillās parvās vocat.*
4. *saevus dominus servum terret.*
5. *agricolae scūta movēbant.*
6. *Rōmānōs nōn vincent.*
7. *mīlitēsne saevī nostram urbem oppugnābunt?*
8. *quis ad templum nōbīscum veniet?*
9. *senēs in agrīs crās erunt.*
10. *mox in nāvibus illīs erimus.*

Exercise 4.18

1. *cantāre potest.*
2. *scībere potes.*
3. *legere nōn potest.*
4. *vidēre nōn possumus.*
5. *currere potestis.*
6. *nāvigāre possunt.*
7. *pugnāre nōn poteram.*
8. *legere nōn poterāmus.*
9. *dormīre nōn poterant.*
10. *potestisne audīre?*
11. *pugnāre poterō.*
12. *cantāre potuerat.*
13. *vidēre posse.*
14. *venīre nōn potuit.*
15. *labōrāre nōn poterāmus.*
16. *poterisne venīre?*
17. *dormīre potuistis.*
18. *regere potuerās.*
19. *tē vidēre, Laelia, nōn possum.*
20. *mē vidēre nōn poterātis.*

Exercise 4.19

1. These boys cannot sing in the temple.
2. Who can see the fields from the town?
3. I shall soon be able to sail along this river.
4. Will the enemy be able to overcome the Romans?
5. These girls were able to run from the town to the sea.
6. Shall we be able to work for a long time in the fields?
7. I am an old man; I can't hurry.
8. This woman can prepare food well.
9. I was not able to write the book.
10. Those leaders were not able to conquer the enemy.

Exercise 4.20

1. *mīlitēsne hostium vidēre potestis?*
2. *hunc librum legere nōn possum.*
3. *in templō cantāre posse cupit.*
4. *ad īnsulam nāvigāre poterunt.*
5. *hostēs superāre potuimus.*
6. *quis hunc mūrum aedificāre poterat?*
7. *diū labōrāre possunt.*
8. *ad urbem currere potest.*
9. *in oppidō manēre potuērunt.*
10. *potestisne cum hostibus pugnāre?*

Chapter 5

Exercise 5.1

1. Won't the Romans always conquer the enemy?
2. Is their fatherland really more beautiful than ours?
3. Weren't the enemy soldiers attacking that town?
4. Won't the farmers work in the fields tomorrow?
5. Did they really sing in the temple yesterday?
6. Isn't this woman very beautiful?
7. Will this boy really hurry into the city?
8. Is it really good to fight with swords and spears?
9. Won't he eat the food in that town?
10. Are the inhabitants of this island really happy?

Exercise 5.2

1. *num agricolae illī in oppidō sunt?*
2. *nōnne magistrī hunc puerum laudābunt?*
3. *num hic equus patris tuī est?*
4. *nōnne hī mīlitēs cum illīs pugnāvērunt?*
5. *num mēcum ad mare curret?*
6. *nōnne illa mulier ad templum festīnat?*
7. *num illī ducēs nāvēs dūcunt?*
8. *nōnne ancillae cibum parant?*
9. *num dē monte cucurrērunt?*
10. *nōnne illī puerī hunc librum lēgērunt?*

Exercise 5.3

1. *postquam discessit*
2. *postquam dormīvimus*
3. *postquam audīvistī*
4. *postquam cucurrī*
5. *postquam festīnāvērunt*
6. *antequam advēnī*
7. *antequam vēnistī*
8. *antequam oppugnāvimus*
9. *antequam appropinquāvērunt*
10. *antequam vīdistis*

Exercise 5.4

1. After they had departed, we read our books.
2. Before the masters came, the boys ran into the temple.
3. Although the old men were tired, they were hurrying into the city.
4. After they had built the wall they were happy.
5. He did not prepare the food before the citizens were present.
6. Although the women were drinking wine, they were miserable.
7. After he had heard the poet Quintus, he praised him greatly.
8. We did not praise that leader, although he led the soldiers well.
9. Before the master came, the maid-servants were frightened.
10. Although I was present, I was not able to hear the king.

Exercise 5.5

1. *ducem, antequam oppidum intrāvit, timēbāmus.*
2. *flūmen, quamquam longissimum erat, nōn erat altum.*
3. *poētam, postquam librum lēgit, cīvēs laudāvērunt.*
4. *antequam urbem intrāvimus, perterritī erāmus.*
5. *magister, quamquam īrātus erat, verba saeva nōn dīxit.*
6. *puerī, postquam in templō cantāvērunt, per agrōs discessērunt.*
7. *urbī, antequam lūx erat, appropinquāvit.*
8. *quamquam cīvēs timuī, in urbe mānsī.*
9. *postquam per mare nāvigāvērunt, ad hanc īnsulam vēnērunt.*
10. *hōs cīvēs, quamquam bonī sunt, nōn amāmus.*

Exercise 5.6

1.   Both the sailors and the farmers came into the town.
2.   The boys, girls, men and women were singing in the temple.
3.   They decided and wanted to fight with the enemy.
4.   Where are the sailors, farmers and soldiers?
5.   We have good leaders of our soldiers and sailors.
6.   The master will praise both the girls and the boys.
7.   We hurried through the towns and through the fields.
8.   Those girls are good and beautiful.
9.   They will soon see both you and us in the town.
10.   The boys are carrying the water and the girls are preparing the food.

Exercise 5.7

1.   *et puerī et puellae in hīs agrīs lūdunt.*
2.   *māter fīliōs fīliāsque magnopere amat.*
3.   *fessī sunt senēs et mulierēs.*
4.   *illī ducēs et malī et saevī erant.*
5.   *magistrī puerōs laudāvērunt dōnaque eīs dedērunt.*
6.   *ad templum et ambulābō et curram.*
7.   *cibum cōnsūmpsimus vīnumque bibimus.*
8.   *mulier pulcherrima et laetissima est.*
9.   *per agrōs festīnāvērunt urbīque appropinquāvērunt.*
10.   *nautae per haec flūmina perque illa maria nāvigābunt.*

N.B. Pupils may of course have chosen different ways of expressing 'and'.

Exercise 5.8

1.   (a)   When Narcissus touched the water with his hand, the ripples caused the reflection to disappear.
      (b)   When he took his hand out of the water, the ripples disappeared and the reflection returned.
      (c)   He could not touch the young man.
      (d)   The young man never replied to Narcissus.
      (e)   He did not want to eat or drink.
      (f)   No, because his body disappeared and in its place they found a very beautiful flower.
      (g)   A very beautiful flower which we still have today in our gardens.
      (h)   Narcissus was punished for his extreme vanity. But did he really deserve to die?

2.   Narcissus therefore gave his right hand to the young man, but when it touched the water, that young man was no longer visible there. Then Narcissus withdrew his right hand, and soon he saw the young man again; and for a long time he watched him; and the young man for a long time watched Narcissus; and Narcissus smiled at the young man; and the young man smiled at Narcissus; but Narcissus could never touch him, (and) the young man never replied to Narcissus; and Narcissus was very miserable. He wanted to eat nothing and to drink nothing; but he was always watching the water in vain and at last he was dead. However when his sisters decided to bury their brother, Narcissus' body was no longer there, but in its place a most beautiful flower appeared; we have this flower in our gardens even today, and we call it the *narcissus*.

3.   (a)   It stands for *dextra* = 'his right hand.'
      (b)   *spectāverat*.
      (c)   *potest*.
      (d)   *respondeō, respondēre, respondī, respōnsum* = I reply.
      (e)   *tangere* = to touch (line 6); *cōnsūmere* = to eat (line 8); *bibere* = to drink (line 8); *sepelīre* = to bury (line 10).
      (f)   *frātrum*.
      (g)   *corpus*.
      (h)   *pulchrior, pulchrior, pulchrius*.

Exercise 5.9

1. Around the island
2. Because of the words
3. Among the citizens
4. After the war
5. Above the land
6. Before the war
7. After the battles
8. Because of the anger
9. Behind the walls
10. Between the girl and the boy

Exercise 5.10

1. *circum mūrōs*
2. *ante bellum*
3. *ante templum*
4. *circum īnsulās*
5. *propter montēs*
6. *super flūmen*
7. *ante noctem*
8. *post noctem*
9. *inter cīvēs*
10. *inter illōs frātrēs*

Exercise 5.11

1. Around the island the sea is fierce.
2. Because of the messengers' words, the citizens will be very happy.
3. There are both good and bad men among the citizens of the city.
4. Who ruled after that king?
5. Above the land the sky is very clear.
6. Before the war the inhabitants were happy.
7. After those battles the soldiers departed.
8. Because of his anger, the maid-servants do not love their new master.
9. Among the women she is the most beautiful.
10. A small boy stood between the king and the queen.

Exercise 5.12

1. *circum templum multī puerī stant.*
2. *quis, propter librōs illīus, Quīntum nōn laudat?*
3. *inter hōs cīvēs multī amīcī meī sunt.*
4. *multī propter bellum miserrimī sunt.*
5. *super urbem nostram multī montēs sunt.*
6. *quis, post nostrum rēgem, terram reget?*
7. *quī* ante hōs incolās hanc īnsulam habitāvērunt?*
8. *inter primum et secundum puerum stat puella.*
9. *multī agrī circum oppidum sunt.*
10. *post hunc puerum sed ante illum vēnit.*

* With apologies for the use of *quis* in the plural.

Exercise 5.13

1. The leader punished no one.
2. The bad master used to give nothing to his slaves.
3. Among these soldiers, no one is savage.
4. I saw no one in the field.
5. Nothing is good there.
6. I shall give those shields to no one.
7. There is nothing in this book.
8. This old man has eaten nothing today.

Exercise 5.14

1. *nēminem in urbe vīdī.*
2. *nihil hīc est.*
3. *hic mīles sōlus nihil ex urbe portāvit.*
4. *nēminī librum dā, Mārce!*
5. *nēminem timeō.*
6. *malus rēx nihil timet.*
7. *nēmō oppidum occupāre cupit.*
8. *nihil in urbe invenient.*

Exercise 5.15

1. Donation: *dōnum* = gift; a donation is a gift.
2. Frustrate: *frūstrā* = in vain; to feel frustrated is to feel that all ones efforts are in vain.
3. Possible: *possum* = I am able; if something is possible, one is able to do it.
4. Annihilate: *nihil* = nothing; to annihilate is to reduce to nothing.
5. Super: *super* = above; super means very good, but is used most commonly as a prefix to mean over or beyond, e.g. superimpose, supersonic etc.

Exercise 5.16

1. *puerī librōs pulchrōs tenēbant.*
2. *nautae saevī oppidum oppugnābant.*
3. *bonī magistrī puellās bonās laudant.*
4. *mulierēs miserae malōs hominēs monēbant.*
5. *equus validus magnum agricolam nōn timet.*
6. *num hic homō parvās puellās timet?*
7. *quamquam dux malus est, bene pugnat.*
8. *postquam ad īnsulam nāvigāvī, fessus eram.*
9. *circum templum current.*
10. *nēmō hīs puerīs dōna dat.*

Exercise 5.17

1.
   (a) A civil war, Romans v. Romans.
   (b) It was very savage; great leaders were overcoming each other, and many citizens were wounding and killing many other citizens.
   (c) Because they used to take their land for themselves.
   (d) *multōsque per annōs* = and for many years.
   (e) After the leaders had conquered each other, Julius Caesar alone remained.
   (f) That he wanted to be a king.
   (g) A king.

2. Once upon a time, Romans were fighting with Romans; there was everywhere a very savage war; great leaders were overcoming great leaders. Many citizens were both wounding and killing many citizens; soldiers were driving out many farmers from their fields and were themselves taking those fields. Death and misery were everywhere and held sway for many years; and after leaders had conquered leaders, one remained, Gaius Julius Caesar: many said about him 'Julius Caesar wishes to be our king.' The Romans had not had kings for many years; they did not like them.

3.
   (a) Nominative plural.
   (b) Accusative plural.
   (c) *superāverant*.
   (d) *necābunt*.
   (e) Accusative plural; it is governed by *per* (+ acc.).
   (f) *ūnīus*.
   (g) *cupīvit*.

Chapter 6

Exercise 6.1

1. These books are better than those.
2. Big shields are better than small ones.
3. A happy master is better than a miserable one.
4. Our soldiers are better than yours.
5. Give this book to the better boy.
6. The teacher praised the better girls.
7. Who wants to walk with better companions?
8. This is the first of the better girls.

Exercise 6.2

1. *hī librī meliōrēs sunt quam illī.*
2. *magna scūta parvīs meliōra sunt.*
3. *laetus dominus miserō melior est.*
4. *nostrī mīlitēs meliōrēs sunt quam vestrī.*

Exercise 6.3

1. *quis melior est quam Caesar?*
2. *haec pulchra flūmina illīs meliōra sunt.*
3. *nōnne melior via est quam haec?*
4. *meliōrēs equī in agrō meliōre stābant.*
5. *hī meliōris senis librī sunt.*
6. *iuvenēs validī malīs meliōrēs sunt.*
7. *agricolae quam nautae meliōrēs sunt.*
8. *num haec meliōra oppida sunt?*
9. *bonī ducēs meliōrēs rēge malō sunt.*
10. *rēx bonus melior quam ducēs malī est.*

Exercise 6.4

1. Is this the best of the boys?
2. Is the best of the boys here?
3. The best temple is in this town.
4. Those men live in the best part of the city.
5. I saw the best farmers in this field.
6. These men praise the best temples.
7. The teacher gave a beautiful book to the best girl.
8. The master wishes to see the best slaves immediately.
9. The angry messengers did not praise the best soldiers.
10. Your parents chose the best teacher for you.

Exercise 6.5

1. *rēgīna ancillam optimam amat.*
2. *estne hoc optimum flūminum?*
3. *ille puer optimus est.*
4. *poēta puellae optimae cantāvit.*
5. *ō rēgum optime! tē laudābimus.*
6. *ad oppidum cum optimīs mīlitibus ambulābitis.*
7. *magister puellārum optimārum est.*
8. *cīvēs optimī verba optima audiunt.*

Exercise 6.6

1. These waves are worse than those.
2. A bad young man is worse than a bad old man.
3. 'What is worse than a bad wind?' says the sailor.
4. Those sailors were saying worse words.
5. Those towns are worse than these.
6. The slaves of the masters are worse than the slaves of the king.
7. The master does not like the worse boys.
8. Those fields belong to (lit. are of) the worse farmers.

Exercise 6.7

1. *illī librī peiōrēs hīs sunt.*
2. *quis peior est quam hic malus mīles?*
3. *saevīne ventī peiōrēs saevīs undīs sunt?*
4. *fessī ducēs quam malī peiōrēs sunt.*
5. *'quid rēge peius est?' dīcēbant Rōmānī.*
6. *magister peiōrēs puerōs nōn laudāvit.*
7. *haec oppida quam illa urbs peiōra sunt.*
8. *hī sunt librī incolārum peiōrum.*

Exercise 6.8

1. These maid-servants are very bad.
2. The worst farmers have the worst fields.
3. Kings are not always very bad.
4. I greatly fear those men, because they are very bad.
5. Do you really love this very bad city?
6. Who praises very bad men?
7. The teacher will not praise the worst girls.
8. The master did not give money to the worst slave.

Exercise 6.9

1. *haec urbs pessima est.*
2. *Mārcus hunc gladium ducī pessimō dedit.*
3. *hōrum senum quis pessimus est?*
4. *illī iuvenēs pessimī sunt.*
5. *pessimum oppidum habitant.*
6. *quid in hāc urbe pessimum est?*
7. *nautae pessimī nāvēs pessimās habēbunt.*
8. *ō mīlitum pessimī, discēdite!*

Exercise 6.10

1. That woman is my wife.
2. What is that? It is a shield.
3. This book is that boy's; he loves it.
4. The slaves are working well; therefore the master will praise them.
5. Order those girls to enter the temple.
6. That city is beautiful; I shall approach it.
7. The enemy wounded the soldier with that arrow; I shall destroy it.
8. The enemy are attacking those towns.
9. Where is Gnaeus? Who has seen him?
10. Sulpicia has seen Gnaeus; ask her.

Exercise 6.11

1. *ubi sunt eae mulierēs? eās vidēre cupiō.*
2. *huncne hominem vidēs? hic gladius eius est.*
3. *eī servī optimī sunt; itaque multa dōna eīs dabimus.*
4. *eī puerī hōs librōs tenent.*
5. *nauta malus est; eum discēdere iubēbō.*
6. *servī bonī sunt; eōs igitur dominīs bonīs dabimus.*
7. *per haec flūmina nāvigābimus.*
8. *laetusne erās, Mārce, propter ea verba?*
9. *in hōc marī multae īnsulae sunt; sed nautae nostrī circum eās nāvigābunt.*
10. *puer nōn bene labōrāvit; eum igitur nōn laudābō.*

Exercise 6.12

1. (a) Brutus and his companions killed him.
   (b) Many were happy, many were angry, and there were savage battles between the two sides.
   (c) Octavian was the son of Julius Caesar's niece, Atia. He was thus his great-nephew.
   (d) (i) His father died; (ii) Brutus and his companions murdered Julius Caesar.
   (e) He was his stepfather.
   (f) That he would be overcome and killed by older and more experienced men.
   (g) To stay with them in order to be safe.
   (h) He ignored it.

2. Julius Caesar did not become (lit. was not) a king; for Brutus, with his companions, killed him; then many people were happy but many were angry; and there were savage battles between those men and these. Caesar had adopted a young man called Octavian and had made him his heir. He was the son of Atia; she was the daughter of Julia, and that Julia was the sister of Julius Caesar. When Octavian was a small boy, his father Octavius died and when Brutus and his companions killed Julius Caesar he was 19 years old. Then both his mother Atia and his mother's new husband, Philippus, used to warn Octavian as follows: 'You are a young man; wicked men will overcome you and kill you. Remain here with us and you will be safe.' But Octavian did not remain with them.

3. (a) Ablative plural of *comes, comitis*, c. = companion.
    (b) *hominēs* = men.
    (c) Pluperfect of *faciō* = I do, make.
    (d) Apposition.
    (e) *necābant*.
    (f) *monēbunt*.
    (g) Imperative (2nd person singular) of *maneō, manēre, mānsī, mānsum* = I remain.
    (h) It means 'here', and not 'this', because the '*ī*' of *hīc* is marked as long.

Exercise 6.13

1. Sulpicia loves Marcus; however she does not love his sisters.
2. Sulpicia loves her (own) sisters.
3. Marcus has a good friend; however he will not defend his (friend's) fatherland.
4. These boys have many friends and they love their (friends') friends.
5. These girls love their (own) parents very much.
6. Marcus is fighting with Gnaeus; the former will overcome the latter.
7. When the Romans wage war with the enemy, the former conquer the latter.
8. The citizens are fleeing from their (own) city.
9. That man will defend their city.
10. These men were defending their (own) fatherland.

Exercise 6.14

1. *suōs librōs mihi trādidit.*
2. *mihi librōs eius trāde, puer.*
3. *gladiōs eōrum cēpimus.*
4. *mīlitēs suās hastās colligent.*
5. *Sulpicia et Laelia hīc sunt; illa laetissima est et haec pulcherrima.*
6. *quis ex urbe suā fugiet?*
7. *rēx cīvēs suōs regit.*
8. *per flūmen eōrum nāvigāmus.*
9. *hās puellās et parentēs eārum amat.*
10. *Mārcus Gāiusque in agrō sunt; hic fessus est, ille nōn est.*

Exercise 6.15

1. Occupy: *occupō* = I seize. When you seize a place, you occupy it.
2. Defend: *dēfendō* = I defend.
3. Collect: *colligō* = I collect; the supine is *collēctum*, from which we get collect and collection.
4. Tradition: *trādō* = I hand over; a tradition is handed over from one generation to another.

5. Fugitive: *fugiō* = I flee; a fugitive is someone who flees.
6. Optimist: *optimus* = best; an optimist always thinks the best of a situation.
7. Pessimist: *pessimus* = worst; a pessimist always thinks the worst of a situation.
8. Circumference: *circum* = around; the circumference is the distance round a circle.

Exercise 6.16

1. *puellae magnae caelum spectābant.*
2. *bona mulier cibum portat.*
3. *dominī servōs laetōs līberābant.*
4. *magistrī īrātī malōs puerōs nōn laudant.*
5. *puerī flūmen sacrum intrābant.*
6. *mīlitēs validī illōs fessōs senēs dēfendunt.*
7. *hī ducēs urbem eius magnam occupāvērunt.*
8. *quid eī magister ostendit?*
9. *cīvēs in urbem suam fugiēbant.*
10. *ostende mihi librum tuum, Laelia; eum vidēre cupiō.*

Exercise 6.17

1. (a) He killed many of them before they could kill him.
    (b) Queen of Egypt.
    (c) A friend of Octavian's.
    (d) A naval battle.
    (e) Merciful.
    (f) Because he was very clever and very tactful.
    (g) Augustus.
    (h) Because he brought peace (*pāx Rōmāna*) to men.

2. Octavian gradually overcame the other leaders; he killed many before they could kill him; at last Antony and
    Cleopatra, the queen of Egypt, alone were left; and Agrippa, a friend of Octavian's, defeated them near
    Actium, a Greek town, in a naval (lit. of ships) battle. Then Octavian alone was the foremost of all men; and
    he pardoned all who had fought with him. He was very clever and although he ruled all, he was very tactful.
    Men no longer called him Octavian but Augustus; he ruled for many years; and Augustus gave a very
    beautiful gift to mankind: Roman peace.

3. (a) *superābat.*
    (b) *necat.*
    (c) *sōlīus.*
    (d) They are in apposition to it.
    (e) *vincō, vincere, vīcī, victum* = I conquer.
    (f) It is its superlative.
    (g) *pulchrius.*
    (h) *hominī.*

Chapter 7

Exercise 7.1

1. *difficilis, -e* = difficult
   Singular

	Masculine	**Feminine**	**Neuter**
Nominative	*difficilis*	*difficilis*	*difficile*
Vocative	*difficilis*	*difficilis*	*difficile*
Accusative	*difficilem*	*difficilem*	*difficile*
Genitive	*difficilis*	*difficilis*	*difficilis*
Dative	*difficilī*	*difficilī*	*difficilī*
Ablative	*difficilī*	*difficilī*	*difficilī*

   Plural

Nominative	*difficilēs*	*difficilēs*	*difficilia*
Vocative	*difficilēs*	*difficilēs*	*difficilia*
Accusative	*difficilēs*	*difficilēs*	*difficilia*
Genitive	*difficilium*	*difficilium*	*difficilium*
Dative	*difficilibus*	*difficilibus*	*difficilibus*
Ablative	*difficilibus*	*difficilibus*	*difficilibus*

2. *facilis, -e* = easy
   Singular

	Masculine	**Feminine**	**Neuter**
Nominative	*facilis*	*facilis*	*facile*
Vocative	*facilis*	*facilis*	*facile*
Accusative	*facilem*	*facilem*	*facile*
Genitive	*facilis*	*facilis*	*facilis*
Dative	*facilī*	*facilī*	*facilī*
Ablative	*facilī*	*facilī*	*facilī*

   Plural

Nominative	*facilēs*	*facilēs*	*facilia*
Vocative	*facilēs*	*facilēs*	*facilia*
Accusative	*facilēs*	*facilēs*	*facilia*
Genitive	*facilium*	*facilium*	*facilium*
Dative	*facilibus*	*facilibus*	*facilibus*
Ablative	*facilibus*	*facilibus*	*facilibus*

3. *fortis, -e* = brave
    Singular

	Masculine	**Feminine**	**Neuter**
Nominative	fortis	fortis	forte
Vocative	fortis	fortis	forte
Accusative	fortem	fortem	forte
Genitive	fortis	fortis	fortis
Dative	fortī	fortī	fortī
Ablative	fortī	fortī	fortī

Plural

	Masculine	**Feminine**	**Neuter**
Nominative	fortēs	fortēs	fortia
Vocative	fortēs	fortēs	fortia
Accusative	fortēs	fortēs	fortia
Genitive	fortium	fortium	fortium
Dative	fortibus	fortibus	fortibus
Ablative	fortibus	fortibus	fortibus

4. *omnis, -e* = all
    Singular

	Masculine	**Feminine**	**Neuter**
Nominative	omnis	omnis	omne
Vocative	omnis	omnis	omne
Accusative	omnem	omnem	omne
Genitive	omnis	omnis	omnis
Dative	omnī	omnī	omnī
Ablative	omnī	omnī	omnī

Plural

	Masculine	**Feminine**	**Neuter**
Nominative	omnēs	omnēs	omnia
Vocative	omnēs	omnēs	omnia
Accusative	omnēs	omnēs	omnia
Genitive	omnium	omnium	omnium
Dative	omnibus	omnibus	omnibus
Ablative	omnibus	omnibus	omnibus

Exercise 7.2

1. The king will give gifts to the brave soldiers.
2. The cruel leader wounded many inhabitants.
3. It is difficult to sing well.
4. The whole temple is sacred.
5. Few citizens were noble.
6. These women were beautiful.
7. He had always made easy journeys.
8. Have they seen the shields of the cruel enemy?
9. These old men are always gloomy.
10. It is always difficult to write well.

Exercise 7.3

1. *hostēs fortēs vincere difficile est.*
2. *omnēs ducēs nōbilēs erant.*
3. *puerī laetī iter facile faciēbant.*
4. *omnis urbs pulcherrima est.*
5. *hī mīlitēs sunt ducum crūdēlium.*
6. *puellae trīstī dōna nōn dedērunt.*
7. *omnēs agricolae bonōs agrōs amant.*
8. *nōbilēs nōn semper fortēs sunt.*
9. *haec verba cantāre facile nōn est.*
10. *omnēs virī et omnēs mulierēs ducēs fortēs habēre cupiunt.*

Exercise 7.4

1. *cīvēs, ubi oppidum hostēs occupāvērunt, perterritī erant.*
2. *iuvenēs, quamquam fessī erant, fortiter pugnābant.*
3. *servō, quod nōn labōrāvit, nihil dedī.*
4. *puerōs puellāsque, ubi bene cantant, laudāmus.*
5. *ducēs, quod mīlitēs fugiēbant, īrātī erant.*
6. *agricolīs, quod mūrōs validōs aedificāvērunt, dōna dedimus.*
7. *ancillae, ubi eās rēgīna vocāvit, celeriter vēnērunt.*
8. *quamquam nihil cōnsūmpserat, ex urbe festīnāvit.*
9. *Aulus, quod comitēs suōs amāvit, cum eīs mānsit.*
10. *ubi senēs templum intrāvērunt, omnēs stetērunt.*

Exercise 7.5

1. The cruel soldiers are taking our swords.
2. The brave boys were standing in front of the little girls.
3. The noble men did not depart from the city without the women.
4. They are throwing arrows into this town.
5. Does not everybody want gold?
6. It is difficult to overcome all the enemy.
7. The farmers work in the fields under the sky.
8. I shall not make the difficult journey without companions.
9. The brave general fought with the wicked men on behalf of the citizens.
10. It is never easy to wage war.

Exercise 7.6

1. *nēmō ā monte discēdet.*
2. *omnēs hominēs ex urbe in templum ambulābant.*
3. *hic senex fortis prō patriā suā pugnat.*
4. *omnis urbs, quod discessērunt hostēs, tūta est.*
5. *malī puerī librōs in viam iaciunt.*
6. *puerī puellaeque sine magistrō librōs legunt.*
7. *omnēs cīvēs ex urbe fugiunt.*
8. *num paucī mīlitēs hōs nōbilēs vīcērunt?*
9. *etiam ille, rēx, sub mūrō manet.*
10. *nōnne hostēs prō templō stant?*

Exercise 7.7

1. (a)   Unpopular.
    (b)   Because he wore little soldier's boots (*caligae*) when he was young.
    (c)   No.
    (d)   *mox* = soon.
    (e)   Because they were very much afraid of him.
    (f)   Very nervous and uncomfortable.
    (g)   Rather sick.

2.   After Augustus came (lit. was) Tiberius, who loved very few people; and very few people loved him. Therefore for many years he lived on the island (of) Capri and used not to come to Rome. After him came (lit. was) Gaius Caesar (all the emperors had the name of Caesar); when he was a little boy, he used to wear little soldier's boots; therefore everyone used to call him Caligula (Bootie). When Caligula first became (lit. began to be) emperor, he was good, but soon, after a disease, he was savage and cruel. Once, when some senators were dining in his home, he began to laugh and could not stop; and when those who were sitting near him asked Caligula 'Why are you laughing?', he replied to them 'Because, if I wish, I can order my slaves to kill you immediately.' Because they very much feared him, they also laughed, but hollowly (lit. pretendedly).

3. (a)   It is its superlative.
    (b)   It is in apposition to it.
    (c)   Because prepositions are not used when going 'to' or 'from' towns and small islands.
    (d)   *omnium*.
    (e)   *esse* = to be (line 7); *rīdēre* = to laugh (line 9); *cessāre* = to stop (line 9); *iubēre* = to order (line 12); *occīdere* = to kill (line 12).
    (f)   *respondērunt*.
    (g)   *eī*.

Exercise 7.8

1.   Publius Pomponius is a friend of Marcus Rabirius'.
2.   Gaius Rabirius gave a gift to Gnaeus Pomponius.
3.   Decimus Pomponius walks into the temple with Publius Pomponius.
4.   This book is Gnaeus Pomponius'.
5.   Where does Manius Rabirius live?
6.   Titus Rabirius is happy because of Lucius Pomponius' words.
7.   Did Quintus Pomponius see Sextus Rabirius yesterday?
8.   Oh, Marcus Rabirius, where is Tiberius Pomponius' sword?
9.   Oh, Publius Pomponius, why don't you praise Servius Rabirius?
10.   Aulus Rabirius will show his fields to Spurius Pomponius.

Exercise 7.9

1.   *A. Pompōnius cum T. Pompōniō nōn pugnāvit.*
2.   *C. Rabīrius Ti. Pompōnium semper laudat.*
3.   *num hic gladius Q. Pompōniī est?*
4.   *ubi est S. Rabīrius?*
5.   *et M. Pompōnius et Cn. Rabīrius librōs scrīpsērunt.*
6.   *ō D. Rabīrī, vīdistīne M' Rabīrium?*
7.   *ō Ser. Pompōnī, hastaene Sp. Rabīrī hae sunt?*
8.   *L. Rabīrius et A. Pompōnius mūrum aedificant.*
9.   *C. Pompōnius prō Q. Rabīriō stat.*
10.   *M. Rabīrius per agrōs P. Pompōniī ambulat.*

Exercise 7.10

1. *ingēns, ingentis* = huge

    Singular

	Masculine	Feminine	Neuter
Nominative	*ingēns*	*ingēns*	*ingēns*
Vocative	*ingēns*	*ingēns*	*ingēns*
Accusative	*ingentem*	*ingentem*	*ingēns*
Genitive	*ingentis*	*ingentis*	*ingentis*
Dative	*ingentī*	*ingentī*	*ingentī*
Ablative	*ingentī*	*ingentī*	*ingentī*

    Plural

	Masculine	Feminine	Neuter
Nominative	*ingentēs*	*ingentēs*	*ingentia*
Vocative	*ingentēs*	*ingentēs*	*ingentia*
Accusative	*ingentēs*	*ingentēs*	*ingentia*
Genitive	*ingentium*	*ingentium*	*ingentium*
Dative	*ingentibus*	*ingentibus*	*ingentibus*
Ablative	*ingentibus*	*ingentibus*	*ingentibus*

2. *audāx, audācis* = bold

    Singular

	Masculine	Feminine	Neuter
Nominative	*audāx*	*audāx*	*audāx*
Vocative	*audāx*	*audāx*	*audāx*
Accusative	*audācem*	*audācem*	*audāx*
Genitive	*audācis*	*audācis*	*audācis*
Dative	*audācī*	*audācī*	*audācī*
Ablative	*audācī*	*audācī*	*audācī*

    Plural

	Masculine	Feminine	Neuter
Nominative	*audācēs*	*audācēs*	*audācia*
Vocative	*audācēs*	*audācēs*	*audācia*
Accusative	*audācēs*	*audācēs*	*audācia*
Genitive	*audācium*	*audācium*	*audācium*
Dative	*audācibus*	*audācibus*	*audācibus*
Ablative	*audācibus*	*audācibus*	*audācibus*

3. *fēlīx, fēlīcis* = fortunate, happy, lucky

Singular

	Masculine	Feminine	Neuter
Nominative	*fēlīx*	*fēlīx*	*fēlīx*
Vocative	*fēlīx*	*fēlīx*	*fēlīx*
Accusative	*fēlīcem*	*fēlīcem*	*fēlīx*
Genitive	*fēlīcis*	*fēlīcis*	*fēlīcis*
Dative	*fēlīcī*	*fēlīcī*	*fēlīcī*
Ablative	*fēlīcī*	*fēlīcī*	*fēlīcī*

Plural

Nominative	*fēlīcēs*	*fēlīcēs*	*fēlīcia*
Vocative	*fēlīcēs*	*fēlīcēs*	*fēlīcia*
Accusative	*fēlīcēs*	*fēlīcēs*	*fēlīcia*
Genitive	*fēlīcium*	*fēlīcium*	*fēlīcium*
Dative	*fēlīcibus*	*fēlīcibus*	*fēlīcibus*
Ablative	*fēlīcibus*	*fēlīcibus*	*fēlīcibus*

4. *sapiēns, sapientis* = wise

Singular

	Masculine	Feminine	Neuter
Nominative	*sapiēns*	*sapiēns*	*sapiēns*
Vocative	*sapiēns*	*sapiēns*	*sapiēns*
Accusative	*sapientem*	*sapientem*	*sapiēns*
Genitive	*sapientis*	*sapientis*	*sapientis*
Dative	*sapientī*	*sapientī*	*sapientī*
Ablative	*sapientī*	*sapientī*	*sapientī*

Plural

Nominative	*sapientēs*	*sapientēs*	*sapientia*
Vocative	*sapientēs*	*sapientēs*	*sapientia*
Accusative	*sapientēs*	*sapientēs*	*sapientia*
Genitive	*sapientium*	*sapientium*	*sapientium*
Dative	*sapientibus*	*sapientibus*	*sapientibus*
Ablative	*sapientibus*	*sapientibus*	*sapientibus*

Exercise 7.11

1. This journey will be easier than that one.
2. We praise the very easy journey.
3. They had entered the huge temple.
4. I shall never love bold men.
5. That very bold young man wounded the soldier with a sword.
6. The gods gave good gifts to the fortunate boy.
7. This mountain is huger than those mountains.
8. Few men have been wiser than Solon.
9. The wall saved this city, although very brave soldiers were attacking it.
10. The brave leader overcame the cruel leader.

Exercise 7.12

1. *cīvēs fortēs mūrum urbis dēfendēbant.*
2. *ventus ingēns templum omne dēlēvit.*
3. *hī senēs, quod cum mīlitibus audācibus pugnant, fortissimī sunt.*
4. *hī iuvenēs, quod in urbe mānsērunt, illīs sapientiōrēs sunt.*
5. *fēlīx puella cibum parat.*
6. *quis hominum sapientissimus est?*
7. *ūnus dux audāx omnēs incolās servāvit.*
8. *parentēs nostrī dē perīculīs omnibus nōs monēbant.*
9. *nōnne crūdēlēs dominī, Aemilia, tē pūnīvērunt?*
10. *num bellum terram hanc omnem dēlēvit?*

Exercise 7.13

1. (a) The Greek and Roman poets wrote about it.
    (b) He was king of Sparta; he was visited by Paris, who took away his (very beautiful) wife, Helen.
    (c) He wanted his brother to help him get his wife back.
    (d) He was king of all the Greeks.
    (e) They gathered together there with their soldiers.
    (f) Because Agamemnon had offended her.
    (g) She did not give them a favourable wind.
    (h) *īrātissimī* = very angry.

2. The Greek and Roman poets have written these things about the Trojan War: Menelaus was the king of Sparta; Paris, the son of Priam, who ruled Troy, visited him. Paris took Menelaus' wife Helen, who was very beautiful, and went away with her to Troy. Menelaus, who wanted to take her back, came to his brother, Agamemnon, and asked him for help. Agamemnon was king of all the Greeks and he called all the leaders to war; these came together with their soldiers near a place called Aulis; they had decided to sail from there to Troy, but Agamemnon had offended the goddess Diana; and the goddess punished all the Greeks in this way: she did not give them a favourable wind, and for a very long time, because they could not sail, the Greeks remained in one place, very angry.

3. (a) *eī.*
    (b) Because a preposition is not used when going 'to' or 'from' towns and small islands.
    (c) *discesserat.*
    (d) *cupiō, cupere, cupīvī, cupītum* = I desire.
    (e) He comes.
    (f) *sine mīlitibus suīs.*
    (g) *eōrum.*
    (h) A (causal) subordinate clause. It is 'tucked in' between *Graecī* and the main verb *manēbant*.

Exercise 7.14

1. *crūdēlis* + (d) cruel: *crūdēlis* = cruel.
2. *difficilis* + (c) difficult: *difficilis* = difficult.
3. *nōbilis* + (b) nobility: *nōbilis* = noble.
4. *omnis* + (e) omnipotent: *omnis* = all; omnipotent means all-powerful. (*potēns* means 'having power'.)
5. *fortis* + (a) fortitude: *fortis* = brave; fortitude means bravery.

Note that *crūdēlis* needed a bit of squashing; serves it right!

Exercise 7.15

1. *bona rēgīna malōs incolās monēbat.*
2. *puerī laetī nova verba cantant.*
3. *nautae saevī pulchram puellam terrēbant.*
4. *agricola validus paucōs equōs līberat.*
5. *magister Graecus cēterōs puerōs laudābat.*
6. *hic locus ingēns trīstior illō est.*
7. *hic audāx puer fēlīcissimus est.*
8. *nōnne miserī senēs parvās puellās monēbant?*
9. *num mīlitēs fortissimī ducem crūdēlissimum superāvērunt?*
10. *num omnēs cīvēs illōs ducēs laudābant?*

Chapter 8

Exercise 8.1

1. Is this sword the bigger man's?
2. Who is greater than Augustus?
3. Is this boy bigger than this girl?
4. That man lives in a big town, but I live in a bigger one.
5. Isn't the sea bigger than rivers?
6. His gifts are bigger than mine.
7. Tomorrow I shall hurry to the mountain with the bigger youths.
8. These spears are the greater men's.
9. Aulus has a bigger sword than I.
10. Laelia does not love her three bigger sisters.

Exercise 8.2

1. *Aulus frātre suō maior est.*
2. *quis maior Alexandrō est?*
3. *tū equum magnum habēs, sed ego maiōrem habeō.*
4. *ad oppidum cum puerīs maiōribus festīnāvī.*
5. *nōnne, agricolae, nostra urbs maior vestrā est?*
6. *mīles, hunc gladium magnum illī iuvenī maiōrī dā.*
7. *illī senēs hīs mulieribus maiōrēs sunt.*
8. *num poēta maior Homērō est?*
9. *illī mīlitēs hastās maiōrēs quam dux noster habent.*
10. *omnēs cīvēs in oppidō maiōre stābant; rīdēbant.*

Exercise 8.3

1. See these men, the greatest of the citizens!
2. Who is the greatest of all poets?
3. That field is the biggest on this island.
4. The greatest temples are in the greatest cities.
5. The greatest leaders live in this land.
6. Who wants to read this the greatest of all books?
7. The enemy threw the biggest arrows into our town.
8. Is that biggest soldier carrying the biggest spears?
9. Isn't this leader a very great soldier?
10. Is this soldier really the greatest leader?

Exercise 8.4

1. *Iūlius Caesar maximus ducum Rōmānōrum erat.*
2. *Aule, suntne in urbe tuā sapientissimī et maximī senēs?*
3. *in patriā meā hoc templum maximum est.*
4. *maximī nautae cum maximīs agricolīs in īnsulā maximā pugnābant.*
5. *maximum librum maximō puerō dabō.*
6. *hī mīlitum maximōrum gladiī sunt.*
7. *senēs dōna magna iuvenibus maximīs dabunt.*
8. *hoc nōmen mulieris maximae est.*
9. *poētam maximum nōs omnēs laudāvimus.*
10. *ducem maximum, quod crūdēlis erat, nēmō amāvit.*

Exercise 8.5

1. Is not this big boy smaller than the horse?
2. This town is smaller than that city.
3. On the small island the temples are rather small.
4. His daughter is smaller than his son / her son.
5. Give the smaller sword to this soldier.
6. Are these youths really smaller than those old men?
7. That man's brother is smaller than his sister.
8. This man is smaller than his own daughter.
9. Aulus and Marcus are smaller than their parents.
10. These rivers are smaller than those.

Exercise 8.6

1. *haec rēgīna minor quam omnēs ancillae est.*
2. *hunc parvum librum, Mārce, puellae minōrī dā.*
3. *duo frātrēs erant: maior et minor.*
4. *illa īnsula minor hāc urbe est.*
5. *quis poētārum hōrum minor est?*
6. *num hic ager agricolae minōris est?*
7. *nōnne hae nāvēs minōrēs illīs sunt?*
8. *māter eius fīliā eius minor est.*
9. *amīcī eius semper eī hastam minōrem dant.*
10. *nōnne illī montēs hīs minōrēs sunt?*

Exercise 8.7

1. This is the smallest of my sons.
2. In this city the smallest girl is the most beautiful.
3. Do the smallest soldiers really fight well?
4. This is the smallest of all our temples.
5. Don't the smallest boys fight very bravely for their fatherland?
6. This master always praises the smallest girls very much.
7. In this town the smallest young men are bigger than the biggest old men.
8. This book is the smallest boy's.
9. The leader sailed to the island in the smallest ship.
10. This is my brother: he is very small.

Exercise 8.8

1. *quis hīc minimus puer est?*
2. *rēgīna dōna minimīs ancillārum dedit.*
3. *nōnne hic puer et frāter eius minimī sunt?*
4. *num hī gladiī iuvenum minimōrum sunt?*
5. *'ō serve, num dominum crūdēlem amās?' 'minimē!'*
6. *etiam minimus poētārum bene scrībere potest.*
7. *'nōnne minimī cīvēs celeriter cucurrērunt?' 'minimē!'*
8. *magister puellīs dōna minima dedit.*

Exercise 8.9

1. (a) 'Who is punishing us in this way?'
   (b) Because Calchas told him he must sacrifice his daughter to the goddess.
   (c) Because his wife Clytemnestra lived there.
   (d) False; the message said that Iphigenia was to marry Achilles, which was untrue.
   (e) To encourage Clytemnestra to come, bringing Iphigenia.
   (f) Because Achilles was the bravest and most noble of the Greek leaders.
   (g) Agamemnon seems to have been keen to do the right thing for the Greek army, and thus consulted the prophet, Calchas. He then wanted to find out what to do to appease the goddess.
   (h) Agamemnon was very devious in deceiving his wife and daughter about the real reason for their journey to Aulis. But then, since he had to get them to come, what choice did he have?

2. At last Agamemnon called the prophet called Calchas and asked him 'Who is punishing us in this way?' He replied 'The goddess Diana is punishing you, because you offended her.' Agamemnon asked again 'What therefore ought I to do now?' The prophet replied 'You must sacrifice your daughter Iphigenia to the goddess.' Agamemnon was very miserable and at last he sent a messenger to Mycenae; his wife Clytemnestra lived there; when he arrived, he said 'Oh! queen, King Agamemnon orders you to come with your daughter Iphigenia to Aulis; for she must marry Achilles.'* Clytemnestra therefore was very happy; for that Achilles was both the bravest and the most noble of the Greek leaders. The queen immediately hurried to Aulis with her daughter.

* In Euripides' play *Iphigenia in Aulis*, Agamemnon subsequently relented and tried, unsuccessfully, to countermand this order.

3. (a) Ablative singular: by name (called).
    (b) The subordinate clause (*quod...offendistī*) is tucked inside the main clause.
    (c) *respondēbit*.
    (d) *filiābus*.
    (e) Because when going 'to' or 'from' towns and small islands, a preposition is not used.
    (f) *coniūnx*.
    (g) The noun *dux* increases in the genitive singular to *ducis*. Although *dux* is a monosyllable, its stem '*duc-*' does not end in two consonants, so it is not covered by the rule affecting monosyllables (see pupil's book, page 45). Its genitive plural *ducum* is therefore regular.
    (h) *festīnāverat*.

Exercise 8.10

1. Oh, my brother, you are both big and strong.
2. Surely they showed all the shields to the leader, didn't they?
3. Surely the boys have read these books, haven't they?
4. Surely the savage waves didn't kill all the sailors, did they?
5. Oh my master, defend your slaves.
6. The enemy have destroyed that town.
7. Oh my son, you sing well.
8. They sent a messenger to the king.
9. Surely the bravest leaders lead us, don't they?
10. Oh my father, why are you very miserable?

Exercise 8.11

1. *nōnne Quīntus, poēta, haec pulcherrima verba scrīpsit?*
2. *nunc, mī puer, validissimus es.*
3. *ventus ingēns mūrum illum dēlēvit.*
4. *nōnne hic mōns altior quam ille est?*
5. *puellae, postquam diū labōrāvērunt, fessae erant.*
6. *num puer parvus hanc sagittam iēcit?*
7. *ō mī fīlī, sapientissimus nōn es.*
8. *Mārcus amīcus Aulī est et eius sorōrem amat.*
9. *Sextus frātrem suum dē perīculīs saepe monuit.*
10. *nōnne, ō mī amīce, ad hoc oppidum mox veniēs?*

Exercise 8.12

1. The young men ran quickly into the city.
2. The old men were fighting bravely with the enemy.
3. The farmers built this wall very quickly.
4. We were defending our city very bravely.
5. These boys hurried into the city as quickly as possible.

Exercise 8.13

1. *hī cīvēs quam celerrimē currunt.*
2. *puellae haec verba bene cantāvērunt.*
3. *iuvenēs urbem fortiter dēfendērunt.*
4. *ventī nāvēs celeriter dēlēvērunt.*
5. *puerī cibum quam celerrimē cōnsūmpsērunt.*

Exercise 8.14

1. Do not sing.
2. Do not shout.
3. Boys, do not play in the temple.
4. Oh master, do not praise the bad young men.
5. Do not wound the wretched horse, oh savage sailor.
6. Oh citizens, do not fear the enemy.
7. Oh queen, do not terrify the maid-servants.
8. Do not flee from the island, inhabitants.
9. Oh my son, do not be a friend of the wicked citizens!
10. Oh young men, do not leave me alone.

Exercise 8.15

1. *nōlī currere.*
2. *nōlīte ambulāre.*
3. *cīvēs, nōlīte hōs equōs occīdere.*
4. *puer parve, nōlī cum puellīs pugnāre.*
5. *agricolae, nōlīte ex agrīs fugere.*
6. *nōlīte in urbe manēre, senēs.*
7. *mī fīlī, nōlī celeriter currere.*
8. *nōlī, ducum fortissime, ex oppidō nostrō discēdere.*
9. *ō mī fīlī, nōlī cibum cōnsūmere.*
10. *ō puerī malī, nōlīte mē terrēre.*

Exercise 8.16

1.
   (a) The truth.
   (b) He was in an impossible position: he had to put his duty to his brother and the Greek army before his duty to his wife and daugher.
   (c) She said 'Do what you must; I am not afraid of death.'
   (d) It was very brave.
   (e) He decided to kill his daughter.
   (f) *sōla* = alone.
   (g) Because he had captured Troy.
   (h) His wife exacted her revenge on him for sacrificing their daughter. Whether he deserved this or not will be a matter of opinion for the pupils to discuss.

2. Clytemnestra and Iphigenia came to Aulis. Agamemnon was afraid to tell his wife the truth; but she soon got to know it. Then the most miserable mother kept saying to her husband 'Do not sacrifice our daughter.' But his brother Menelaus* said 'Get (lit. take) my wife back!' and the Greek leaders kept shouting, 'Lead us, lead us without delay to Troy.' Then Iphigenia said to Agamemnon 'Oh father, do what you must do; I do not fear death.' And the most miserable father decided to kill her. And immediately there was a favourable wind. Then the Greeks sailed to Troy, but Clytemnestra came back to Mycenae alone, very wretched and very angry. And when, after ten years, Agamemnon captured Troy and returned happy to his fatherland, his wife immediately killed him in the bath.

* In fact, in Euripides' play *Iphigenia in Aulis*, Menelaus dropped his request, but Agamemnon dared not disband the army.

3.
   (a) Because there are two subjects (*Clytaemnēstra et Īphigenīa*).
   (b) Nominative feminine singular.
   (c) Accusative neuter singular.

(d)   *clāmāverant.*
(e)   *dīcet.*
(f)   *fuērunt.*
(g)   Because when going 'to' or 'from' towns and small islands, a preposition is not used.
(h)   *sōlīus.*

Exercise 8.17

1.   When I arrived, I found nothing.
2.   When the enemy came to the city, the citizens escaped from them.
3.   The wicked sailors have captured our women; and we want to lead them back as quickly as possible.
4.   Will the girls escape from the sailors?
5.   The brave leader received a very beautiful gift.
6.   Did you not find much money in the town?
7.   The women gave the men both food and wine.
8.   We shall lead the boys back safe from the enemy as quickly as possible.
9.   After the enemy had approached the city, the citizens decided to escape from them.
10.   Did you really find gold in the field?

Exercise 8.18

1.   *num hostēs, Tite, quam celerrimē effūgistī?*
2.   *hodiē multa dōna accipiam.*
3.   *hanc parvam puellam herī in agrō invēnī.*
4.   *crās in oppidum adveniēmus.*
5.   *quis senēs ex īnsulā redūxit?*
6.   *servī īram dominī effūgērunt.*
7.   *comitēs meī pecūniam multam herī accēpērunt.*
8.   *in oppidum mēcum advēnit.*
9.   *mulierēs Rōmam crās redūcam.*
10.   *cēterās hastās post proelium invēnimus.*

Exercise 8.19

1.   Invent: *inveniō* = I find. To invent is to find a new way of achieving something.
2.   Accept: *accipiō* = I receive. To receive is to accept (from supine *acceptum*).
3.   Audacious: *audāx* = bold. Audacious means bold.
4.   Felicity: *fēlīx* = fortunate; felicity means happiness (good fortune).

Exercise 8.20

1.   *bonī dominī servōs monēbant.*
2.   *magistrī īrātī malōs puerōs nōn laudant.*
3.   *parvae puellae multum aurum habent.*
4.   *agricolae validī mūrum altum aedificābant.*
5.   *poēta templum pulchrum spectābat.*
6.   *hostēs crūdēlēs urbem oppugnābant.*
7.   *herī ventī saevī templa dēlēvērunt.*
8.   *incolae perterritī mīlitēs effūgērunt.*
9.   *dominī malōs servōs pūnīvērunt.*
10.   *iuvenēs fortissimī senēs miserōs servāvērunt.*

Chapter 9

Exercise 9.1

Present tense

1st person singular	*eō*	I go, am going, do go
2nd person singular	*īs*	You (sing.) go, are going, do go
3rd person singular	*it*	He, she, it goes, is going, does go
1st person plural	*īmus*	We go, are going, do go
2nd person plural	*ītis*	You (plur.) go, are going, do go
3rd person plural	*eunt*	They go, are going, do go

Imperfect tense

1st person singular	*ībam*	I was going, used to go
2nd person singular	*ībās*	You (sing.) were going, used to go
3rd person singular	*ībat*	He, she, it was going, used to go
1st person plural	*ībāmus*	We were going, used to go
2nd person plural	*ībātis*	You (plur.) were going, used to go
3rd person plural	*ībant*	They were going, used to go

I leave it to you whether or not you ring your pupils at 3.00 a.m. to make sure that they know these tenses.

Exercise 9.2

1. *exeō*: as above, with addition of prefix *ex-,* and meanings: I go out etc.
2. *ineō*: as above, with addition of prefix *in-,* and meanings: I go in etc.
3. *pereō*: as above, with addition of prefix *per-,* and meanings: I perish etc.
4. *redeō*: as above, with addition of prefix *red-,* and meanings: I go back etc.
5. *trānseō*: as above, with addition of prefix *trāns-,* and meanings: I go across etc.

Exercise 9.3

1. The citizens were going out of the town quickly.
2. You were all going into the field.
3. The boys and girls return from the island.
4. Who was going around the temple yesterday?
5. Were the slaves really crossing the river without their master?
6. Oh young man, aren't you going with me to Rome?
7. Many men die in a great war.
8. Sextus and I are crossing into the town.
9. Our parents are at last returning to us.
10. Your leader was entering the battle.

Exercise 9.4

1. *amīcī meī Rōmam mēcum redeunt.*
2. *omnēs puerī in templum inībant.*

3.   *circum oppidum eunt.*
4.   *flūmen saepe trānsīmus.*
5.   *in monte perībātis.*
6.   *nōnne ex agrīs, Aule, exībās?*
7.   *num mīlitēs ad urbem sine duce redībant?*
8.   *nunc in agrōs eō et ibi labōrābō.*
9.   *Mārcus in īnsulam magnam saepe trānsībat.*
10. *multī cīvēs proelium ineunt.*

Exercise 9.5

1.   (a) Because he wanted to behead it with one blow.
     (b) It could either mean 'He ordered his slaves to kill many men'; or 'He ordered many men to kill his slaves'. It is more likely that he would be giving orders such as this to his slaves, rather than ordering unspecified people to murder his slaves.
     (c) To occupy Britain.
     (d) He had *shown* Britain to the Romans but had not occupied it.
     (e) He clearly held them in very low esteem.
     (f) A soldier called Cassius Chaerea killed him.
     (g) He called him a monster.

2.   Once upon a time Caligula, when he was angry, said 'All of Rome ought to have had a single neck.' For he wanted to behead it all with one wound. He ordered his slaves to kill many men; he punished many men very cruelly. Once he sent his soldiers into Gaul, to the sea. Men said 'Now he will occupy Britain.' For Julius Caesar had shown Britain to the Romans; however he had not occupied it. But soon Caligula ordered those soldiers to bring back, not victory, but sea-shells. He decided to make his horse, called Incitatus, a consul. Soon a soldier called Cassius Chaerea killed Caligula. Suetonius, who wrote about his life, called Caligula a monster.

3.   (a) *ūnīus.*
     (b) Ablative singular of *vulnus*.
     (c) Superlative adverb.
     (d) Accusative singular, after *in* + acc.
     (e) *iubēbit.*
     (f) *suum* = his (own).
     (g) Present infinitive of *faciō*. Other examples: *habēre* = to have (line 2); *dētruncāre* = to behead (line 3); *occīdere* = to kill (line 4); *reportāre* = to bring back (line 9).

Exercise 9.6

1.   These young men always praise themselves.
2.   Those citizens quickly moved themselves from the battle.
3.   This boy by chance wounded himself with a sword.
4.   Marcus was telling himself the words of the poet.
5.   When the enemy conquered him, that leader killed himself.
6.   They will not give themselves gold tomorrow.
7.   Will he not free himself from the wicked master.
8.   Narcissus caught sight of himself in the water.
9.   Although he was tired, Aulus defended himself bravely.
10. What did that old man carry with him?

Exercise 9.7

1. *Narcissus sē amāvit.*
2. *hī mīlitēs novōs gladiōs sibi dedērunt.*
3. *hic senex multōs librōs sēcum in urbem portāvit.*
4. *Gāius et Sextus semper sē laudābunt.*
5. *cūr Narcissus in flūmine sē spectat?*
6. *puellae sibi verba poētae dīcunt.*
7. *in aquā herī sē vīdit.*
8. *dux trīstis hostibus sē trādidit.*
9. *hic senex, ubi labōrat, sibi cantat.*
10. *herī hic parvus puer sē forte vulnerāvit.*

Exercise 9.8

1. **Future tense**

1st person singular	*exībō*	I shall go out
2nd person singular	*exībis*	you (sing.) will go out
3rd person singular	*exībit*	he, she, it will go out
1st person plural	*exībimus*	we shall go out
2nd person plural	*exībitis*	you (pl.) will go out
3rd person plural	*exībunt*	they will go out

   Perfect tense

1st person singular	*exiī*	I have gone out, went out
2nd person singular	*exīstī*	you (sing.) have gone out, went out
3rd person singular	*exiit*	he, she, it has gone out, went out
1st person plural	*exiimus*	we have gone out, went out
2nd person plural	*exīstis*	you (pl.) have gone out, went out
3rd person plural	*exiērunt*	they have gone out, went out

2. As above, substituting *in-* for *ex-*; I shall go in, enter etc.
3. As above, substituting *per-* for *ex-*; I shall perish, etc.
4. As above, substituting *red-* for *ex-*; I shall go back, etc.
5. As above, substituting *trāns-* for *ex-*; I shall go across, etc.

Exercise 9.9

1. Soon we shall cross into the fields.
2. At last you went into this town.
3. Did that old man return to the island.
4. I shall cross the river here.
5. Many citizens suddenly went out of the city.
6. The boys and girls will go into the temple.
7. The brave soldiers had perished in the battle.
8. Tomorrow we shall all return to the fields.
9. Will the women really go around the mountain?
10. Won't all the horses go out of the field?

Exercise 9.10

1. *crās in templum inībimus.*
2. *herī mīlitēs ex urbe exiērunt.*
3. *puerī puellaeque in agrōs trānsiērunt.*
4. *ego et Aulus in oppidum iniimus.*
5. *iuvenēs ad flūmen redierant.*
6. *mulierēs viam quam celerrimē trānsiērunt.*
7. *num ex templō crās exībunt?*
8. *Laelia, ad montem īstī?*
9. *ego et Sulpicia circum agrum iimus.*
10. *nōnne, Mārce, herī redīstī?*

Exercise 9.11

1. (a) The fact that he was ugly and freakish.
   (b) Claudius hid behind some curtains in the palace. He was discovered because his feet were sticking out.
   (c) He thought he was going to be killed.
   (d) The soldiers swore allegiance to him.
   (e) He often behaved wisely, he did many things well and he was the first of the Romans to add a large part of Britain to the empire.
   (f) Agrippina was Claudius' fourth wife, so he obviously did not find a long and happy marriage easy to achieve.
   (g) She was thought ambitious enough to murder Claudius and make her son Nero emperor.
   (h) Nero became emperor.

2. After Caligula was Claudius, his paternal uncle. His relatives either neglected or made fun of this man, who was ugly and freakish. Already middle-aged, when Chaerea killed Caligula, he hid himself in the Palace between curtains, terrified. However a soldier, who had rushed with his companions into the Palace, caught sight of his feet; and he led him to the soldiers' camp. There the soldiers did not kill him, as he had feared, but swore allegiance to him; thus Claudius became (lit. was) the emperor. Although he punished the guilty cruelly, he often behaved wisely; he did many things well. Claudius, first of the Romans, added a large part of Britain to the Roman empire. At last his fourth wife Agrippina, who was already the mother of Nero, perhaps killed him, with the help of a mushroom; and after him the emperor was Nero.

3. (a) *occīdet.*
   (b) No; he had gone with his companions.
   (c) Pluperfect.
   (d) *nōmina* = names.
   (e) Genitive singular; Claudius.
   (f) They form a subordinate clause which is tucked in between *is* and the main verb *gerēbat*.
   (g) A reflexive pronoun.
   (h) *erit.*

Exercise 9.12

1. Thirteen girls did/made this.
2. Twelve boys were fighting with six young men.
3. Quintus has written eleven books.
4. Lucius is the master of fourteen slaves.
5. I gave twenty books to the twenty girls.
6. Nineteen soldiers entered the town.
7. In this town there are seventeen large roads.
8. Fifteen horses are standing in these fields.
9. Eighteen men are singing in the temple.
10. Sixteen citizens built these walls.

Exercise 9.13

1. *sēdecim et trēs ūndēvīgintī sunt.*
2. *decem et decem vīgintī sunt.*
3. *quīndecim et duo septendecim sunt.*
4. *ūndecim et septem duodēvīgintī sunt.*
5. *duodecim et duo quattuordecim sunt.*
6. *tredecim et quattuor septendecim sunt.*

Exercise 9.14

1. *ūndecim puerī in illā viā sunt.*
2. *duodecim mulierēs circum templum ībant.*
3. *nōnne illōs quīndecim senēs vidēre potes, Sulpicia?*
4. *multī mīlitēs cum ūndēvīgintī cīvibus pugnābant.*
5. *sex fortēs iuvenēs septendecim nautās superāvērunt.*
6. *hī ducēs tredecim urbēs oppugnāvērunt.*
7. *quattuordecim agricolae in agrīs suīs labōrant.*
8. *sēdecim incolae iter longum faciēbant.*
9. *num omnēs duodēvīgintī puellās, Mānī, audīre potes?*
10. *montī cum vīgintī comitibus appropinquāvī.*

Exercise 9.15

1. *exeō* + (a) exit: *exeō* = I go out; an exit is a way of going out.
2. *pereō* + (d) perish: *pereō* = I die; to perish is to die.
3. *trānseō* + (b) transit: *trānseō* = I go across; to be in transit is to be going across from one location to another.
4. *dormiō* + (c) dormitory: *dormiō* = I sleep; a dormitory is a room in which one sleeps.

Exercise 9.16

1. *bonus dominus servōs fessōs laudābat.*
2. *incolae validī mūrum magnum aedificābant.*
3. *ancillae laetae novam rēgīnam amant.*
4. *magistrī īrātī malōs puerōs monēbant.*

5. *fēminae miserae bella longa timent.*
6. *multī autem mīlitēs in oppidum ruērunt.*
7. *ducēs cōpiās sēcum in urbem dūxērunt.*
8. *senēs propter īram rēgis perterritī erant.*
9. *amīcus meus mēcum Rōmam ībit.*
10. *iuvenēs fortēs multa prō parvīs puellīs dīxērunt.*

Exercise 9.17

1. That man has more gold than the king.
2. Who has more books than he (has)?
3. I gave spears to more boys than (I did) to young men.
4. More inhabitants have more money.
5. That farmer drinks more wine than this one.
6. Most citizens do not love wars.
7. That leader went into the city with very many companions.
8. The old men said more than the young men.

Exercise 9.18

1. *plūra verba crās vōbīs dīcam.*
2. *Sulpicia, plūs cibī nōbīs dā.*
3. *plūs īrae quam virtūtis in illō virō est.*
4. *Mārcus plūs aurī quam Aulus habet.*
5. *hic agricola equōs plūrimōs habet.*
6. *haec terra plūrēs urbēs quam illa habet.*
7. *plūrimōs librōs puellīs sapientibus dabō.*
8. *plūrimī incolae plūs pecūniae cupiunt.*

Chapter 10

Exercise 10.1

(a) Orpheus was the son of Calliopea.
(b) Men and wild beasts stood around him, rivers stopped flowing, and mountains and trees approached him.
(c) Eurydice; she was a very beautiful and very sweet nymph.
(d) A snake bit her and killed her.
(e) He was very miserable.
(f) To lead Eurydice back from the Underworld to the world.
(g) To go into that place.
(h) As a savage and gloomy place.

Translation of passage (not required of pupil):

Orpheus, the son of Calliopea, foremost of the Muses, lived in Thrace; when he sang, not only men but also wild beasts stood around him, rivers no longer flowed, mountains and trees approached him; for everyone and everything wanted to hear him. His wife, called Eurydice, was a very beautiful and very sweet nymph; he loved her greatly; and she loved him; they were very happy, the two of them (lit. both he and she); but a snake bit her and killed her; Orpheus was very sad at her death; he very much wanted to lead her back into the world from the Underworld. Therefore he decided very bravely to enter that savage and gloomy place.

Exercise 10.2

When Orpheus arrived in the Underworld, even there he overcame everyone with his songs; he softened not only Charon, who used to convey the dead in his boat into the Underworld, but also Cerberus, a very fierce dog, who had three heads; moreover, when Orpheus sang, all the dead and all the monsters and freaks no longer howled but listened to him, happy and quiet. At last the king of the Underworld, Pluto, and the queen, Proserpina, said these words to him: 'It is permitted to you to lead your wife back out of the darkness of the Underworld into the world; you go first, and she will go behind you; but do not look back at her before she is (lit. will be) on the earth: if you (will) do this, you will never see her alive again.

Exercise 10.3

(a) Pluperfect of *redeō*: he had returned.
(b) Dative singular of *lūx, lūcis*, f. = light.
(c) *nōn poterat*.
(d) *illud*.
(e) Accusative plural; because it is the object of *cantābat*.
(f) *iaciō, iacere, iēcī, iactum* = I throw.
(g) The use of a preposition tells us that it is not a *small* island.
(h) It would change to *cantābit*.

Translation of passage (not required of pupil):

Very happy, Orpheus was going out of the Underworld; and behind him was going Eurydice; and now he had returned into the world, and now behind him Eurydice was approaching the light. But Orpheus could not do what Pluto and Proserpina had ordered: and alas! when Eurydice was not yet in the world, he looked back! Immediately she was no longer visible. Then Orpheus wandered, very miserable, through the lands and sang very sad songs. At last, women who were worshipping the god Bacchus, killed him, because he preferred Apollo to Bacchus; and they threw his head into the river Hebrus; and the river carried the head to the sea, and the waves conveyed it to the island of Lesbos; and it was always singing a sad but beautiful song.

Exercise 10.4

(i) *bona rēgīna fessās ancillās laudābat.*

(ii) *parvī puerī longum bellum timent.*

Exercise 10.5

(a) Because he had killed his brother and another citizen.

(b) Because it was she who had fallen in love with him.

(c) He could not do it, because Bellerophon had come as a suppliant.

(d) He ordered Bellerophon to take a letter to his wife's father, the king of Lycia; in the letter he wrote that its bearer had planned to take for himself the king's daughter, and that he should thus be killed.

(e) He was his son-in-law.

(f) He did not wish to kill Bellerophon because he was a guest.

(g) To destroy the Chimaera.

(h) A very huge and very savage monster.

Translation of passage (not required of pupil):

Bellerophon, a young man, lived in Corinth; but when he killed both his brother and another citizen, he fled to Tiryns as a suppliant to king Proetus; when this man's wife saw the young man, she immediately loved him, but when he rejected her, she, very angry, said to her husband 'Bellerophon wants to have me for himself; kill him.' But Proetus could not himself kill him, because he was a suppliant; therefore he ordered him to take a sealed letter to his wife's father, the king of Lycia, who was called Iobates; in that letter he wrote these words: 'Kill the man who gives (lit. will give) this letter to you; for he planned to have my wife, your daughter, for himself.' Iobates too did not himself want to kill a guest; therefore he said to Bellerophon: 'I ask you this; make me happy; destroy the Chimaera.' The Chimaera was a very huge and very savage monster.

Exercise 10.6

Therefore Bellerophon wanted to destroy the Chimaera; it had three parts: one part was a lioness, another part was a she-goat, the third (part was) a dragon; it breathed fire. But Minerva gave him a winged horse called Pegasus; with the help of Pegasus, Bellerophon flew over the Chimaera and overcame it with many arrows. However Iobates was not only ungrateful but ordered Bellerophon to undergo many other dangers and to overcome many other men; and with Pegasus' help he overcame all of them. At last Iobates ordered his soldiers to kill the young man; but Neptune saved him; he (lit. who) kept sending great waves on to the plain where the king's palace stood. Afterwards Iobates said to Bellerophon 'What I have read about you is not true; I have sinned against you greatly; forgive me.'

Exercise 10.7

(a) *dabat*

(b) Ablative singular of *auxilium, auxiliī*, n. = help

(c) *deus*

(d) *dīcet*

(e) *capiō, capere, cēpī, captum* = I take, capture

(f) *post mē* = after me (line 3); *ad montem* = to the mountain (lines 4-5); *sub caudā* = under the tail (line 8); *ad terram* = to the land (line 9); *īn spīnās* = into the thorns (lines 10-11); *per terrās* = through the lands (line 12)

(g) Perfect/past tense; wounded

(h) Accusative, masculine plural of *is, ea, id* = that

Translation of passage (not required of pupil):

Then Iobates gave Bellerophon his other daughter as a wife; her name was Philonoe; and Iobates said to Bellerophon: 'You will be king of Lycia after me.' Then Bellerophon behaved like a king and was very happy; but once upon a time he decided to fly to Mount Olympus, with the help of Pegasus; for the immortal gods lived there; and Bellerophon now said to himself: 'You are similar to an immortal god.' Therefore Jupiter ordered a gadfly to sting Pegasus under his tail; he suddenly raised himself and threw Bellerophon to the ground. Then Jupiter took Pegasus and ordered him to carry his thunderbolts. However Bellerophon fell into thorns; and these wounded him greatly; and afterwards he wandered alone through the lands, and did not wish to greet other men; thus the gods used to punish those who said to themselves: 'You are similar to a god.'

Exercise 10.8

    (i)   *validōs nautās timēmus.*
    (ii)   *parvī puerī magnōs equōs spectābant.*

Exercise 10.9

    (a)   Because he was the king of Athens.
    (b)   The sandals and sword of Aegeus.
    (c)   He moved the stone and took the sword and sandals to Athens.
    (d)   Sinis was a very savage man who lived near Corinth.
    (e)   Anyone passing through his fields.
    (f)   He asked them to hold the top of the tree (which he was holding down); he then let go, and the tree flew up, sending the victims flying into the air. When they hit the ground, they died.
    (g)   Yes, because he had to bend and hold down the tree, which flew up when he let go.
    (h)   Theseus overcame him and killed him.

Translation of passage (not required of pupil):

Aegeus and Aethra were Theseus' parents; they lived in the city of Troezen. But soon Aegeus, who was king of Athens, returned to Athens; before he departed, he left his sword and his sandals under a rock and he said to his wife: 'When the boy is (lit. will be) able to move the rock, order him to carry that which is under it to Athens.' When he was sixteen years old, Theseus moved the rock, and carried his father's sword and sandals to Athens. Near Corinth lived Sinis, a very savage man: he used to bend the top of a tree down to the ground and if anyone by chance was journeying through the fields, he would ask him for help; then, when that person was holding the top of the tree, he would suddenly let go: the tree with the man would fly as quickly as possible to the sky: and it would throw the man to the ground and kill him. Sinis wanted to kill Theseus in this way, but Theseus himself overcame him and killed him.

Exercise 10.10

Theseus was now approaching Attica; and when he came to Megara, Sciron wanted to kill him; that man used to sit on a cliff and order those who crossed to wash his feet; and when they had done this, he used to kick them down (lit. throw down with his feet) from the cliff into the sea. There lived there very huge tortoises; and these used immediately to eat the bodies of those whom Sciron threw down; in this way he wanted to kill Theseus; but Theseus fought with him and threw him himself into the sea. Then Theseus came into Attica; there the brigand Procrustes used to kill his guests in this way: he had a bed, in which the guest used to sleep; he used to cut off parts of the limbs of the guest who was longer than the bed, (and) pull asunder the limbs of the (guest) who was shorter than the bed; in this way he used to kill his guests; however in this way Theseus overcame the brigand and killed him.

Exercise 10.11

(a)   Either a town or a small island, because there is no preposition before it.
(b)   Pluperfect.
(c)   Present infinitive: *esse* = to be (line 3).
(d)   Conspicuous: *cōnspiciō* = I catch sight of; conspicuous means easily visible.
(e)   *post patrem* = after his father (lines 2-3); *in quō* = in which (line 9); *ā labrīs* = from the lips (line 9); *ad terram* = to the ground (line 10); *cum fīliō* = with her son (line 11); *in exilium* = into exile (lines 11-12); *in multīs locīs* = in many places (line 13).
(f)   *clamābit.*
(g)   *crūdēlibus.*
(h)   Men.

Translation of passage (not required of pupil):

At last Theseus arrived in Athens; there Aegeus, his father, had married Medea; they had had a son; the mother wanted this son to be king of Athens after his father; she immediately recognised Theseus and said to her husband: 'This man is a friend of our enemies and wants to kill us; but I shall give him poisoned wine before he does (lit. will do) it.' And Theseus was on the point of drinking the wine; but his father suddenly caught sight of his own sword, which Theseus was holding, and immediately snatched the cup in which the wine was away from his lips and threw it down to the ground. Then he shouted to Theseus, 'You are my son and my heir.' He sent Medea with her son into exile. Afterwards Theseus killed a very savage bull, which lived at Marathon. In this way in many places he freed men from very cruel monsters, and good men all praised him greatly and loved him.

Exercise 10.12

(i)   *magnum oppidum oppugnāmus.*
(ii)   *parvae puellae poētam bonum monēbant.*

Exercise 10.13

¹P	²O	³S	⁴T	⁵Q	U	A	⁶M

(crossword grid)

Across/Down grid:

Row 1: P O S T Q U A M
Row 2: O · U I U S · O
Row 3: S T A B I · · X
Row 4: T U · I D E S ·
Row 5: E Q U · N U M
Row 6: A U T · V I A
Row 7: · E A E M · I N
Row 8: M · C A T I S
Row 9: E · E C U N · U
Row 10: A N T E Q U A M